Beyond Remote-Controlled Childhood

Teaching Young Children in the Media Age

Diane E. Levin

National Association for the Education of Young Children
Washington, DC

National Association for the
Education of Young Children
1313 L Street NW, Suite 500
Washington, DC 20005-4101
202-232-8777 • 800-424-2460
www.naeyc.org

NAEYC Books

Chief Publishing Officer
Derry Koralek

Editor-in-Chief
Kathy Charner

Director of Creative Services
Edwin C. Malstrom

Managing Editor
Mary Jaffe

Senior Editor
Holly Bohart

Senior Graphic Designer
Malini Dominey

Associate Editor
Elizabeth Wegner

Editorial Assistant
Ryan Smith

Through its publications program, the National Association for the Education of Young Children (NAEYC) provides a forum for discussion of major issues and ideas in the early childhood field, with the hope of provoking thought and promoting professional growth. The views expressed or implied in this book are not necessarily those of the Association or its members.

Credits
Cover design: *Edwin Malstrom*
Cover photo: *Ellen B. Senisi*
Copy editor: *Lisa Cook*

Library of Congress Control Number: 2013941808
ISBN: 978-1-928896-98-2
NAEYC Item #372

About the Author

 **Diane E. Levin,** Ph.D., a professor of early childhood education at Wheelock College in Boston, has been involved in training early childhood professionals for more than 30 years. Most recently she has taught courses on the meaning and development of play and on how early childhood programs can help communities affected by war and conflict heal. These courses have included service learning work in Northern Ireland as well as a summer institute, Media Madness.

Diane is an internationally recognized expert who helps professionals and parents deal with the effects of various societal forces—such as violence, poverty, media and commercial culture, gender stereotypes, and high-stakes testing—on children, families, and schools. She advocates widely on issues related to children's well-being and is a cofounder of Teachers Resisting Unhealthy Children's Entertainment, Defending the Early Years, and the Campaign for a Commercial-Free Childhood. She is the author or coauthor of six other books, including *So Sexy So Soon, Teaching Young Children in Violent Times,* and *The War Play Dilemma.* Diane is a frequent keynote speaker and workshop presenter.

Dedication

To the Steering Committee members (past and present) of Teachers
Resisting Unhealthy Children's Entertainment (TRUCE), who have
worked with me since 1995 to prepare materials that
help parents of young children make good
decisions about the media, technology,
and toys in their children's lives

Acknowledgments

I offer my deep thanks and appreciation to the many parents and professionals whose stories and experiences with young children around media and technology inform almost every page of this book. Special thanks go to the following individuals for so generously sharing their stories and expertise with me:

- Camille Adler for sharing her experiences with children on media-related issues
- Sara Adler for contributing the letter to families about birthday parties for girls in Box 3.1
- Connie Biewald and Sarah Napier for sharing the media literacy curriculum activities they developed with elementary school children and for contributing the class discussion in Box 6.5 and the children's advertising illustrations in Box 9.5
- Kris Krueger Blue for sharing experiences and photographs (including the two in Chapter 7) of her outstanding work with children at Clapboardtree Nursery School to counteract the impact of media
- Lori Pino Botolino for sharing her work on media and media culture with children and supplying the dialogue with Henry in Chapter 2; the TV-viewing rules in Boxes 6.8, 6.9, 6.10, and 6.11; the children's drawings of alternatives to watching TV in Box 6.12, the letters in Box 9.7; and the family homework activity in Box 10.10
- Blakely Bundy for creating a screen-free week in her community that provides a model for us all
- Karen Economopoulos for writing the original version of the letter to families in Box 8.2
- Mary Finucane for contributing the insights from her own experiences with her young daughter and princess play in Box 5.5
- Lani Gerson for sharing her knowledge of children's books to use in working meaningfully with children in the media age
- Christine Gerzon for contributing the mouse activity in Box 6.11
- Nancy Howe at the Bing Nursery School in Palo Alto, California, for sharing her efforts to deal with a range of media issues in her work with children and families and for contributing, along with Diana Suskind, the stones and technology experience in Box 7.5
- Karen Kosko for providing expert assistance in selecting and annotating the Resources section on recommended children's books
- Margaret LaBonte for sharing materials on her efforts to promote a screen-free week in the Boston school community, including the log in Box 6.16
- Geralyn McLaughlin for offering multiple examples of work with children, colleagues, and families on media education issues at the Mission Hill School, including a screen-free week, and for supplying the following accounts: the "popular girls" table in Chapter 1, age progression in Box 3.2, the gift of play in Chapter 7, the toy lending library in Box 10.7, the article in Box 10.11, and the parents' night in Box 10.12

- Chris Morton and members of Youth Enlightening Youth for supplying the letter to kindergarten children in Box 8.5A
- Helen Moschapidakis for sharing her insights and breakthroughs as she has parented her children in the media age
- Ruth Schreier and Megan Thomas for sharing the account of the news curriculum they created in Box 9.3
- Sarah Owens Smith for supplying the account of her action research on the role of recess in reducing off-task behavior in Box 7.6
- Danielle Socier for writing the letter to parents about *Iron Man* in Box 10.9
- John Surr for his vital assistance in preparing the Resources section
- Diana Suskind for sharing her enthusiasm as a devoted promoter of creative play with children and for contributing, along with Nancy Howe, the stones and technology account in Box 7.5
- Tracey Wright for sharing the story about a parent and homework in Box 10.6
- Many other unnamed teachers and parents for willingly sharing their stories with me through the decades, stories that have helped shape my understanding and the content of this book. Some of their accounts are used in this book. In some cases, aspects of their stories have been combined.

Extra-special thanks goes to my deeply committed colleagues and kindred spirits in activism on behalf of children's well-being, without whose wisdom and insight I would not have been able to write this book: TRUCE Steering Committee Members (present and past) Kathy Clunis D'Andrea, Sarae Decoster-Pacetta, Irene Diamond, Donna DiFillippo, Christine Gerzon, Hugh Hanley, Geralyn McLaughlin, Mary Ross, Kathy Roberts, and Honey Schnapp, along with Campaign for a Commercial-Free Childhood staff members Susan Linn, Josh Golin, and Shara Drew. I appreciate the input of the TRUCE members as well as Nancy Carlsson-Paige for their contributions to the letter that appears in Box 8.5B.

Deep thanks to Nancy Carlsson-Paige, dear friend and colleague, who has been my collaborator from the beginning of my work on the impact of media culture on young children, and with whom I have continued to collaborate to create a more just and caring world for children.

Appreciation goes to my faculty colleagues and administrators at Wheelock College who put up with all the times I was distracted because I was lost in the creation of this book—especially Gail Dines, from whom I have learned so much, and with whom I have taught the annual summer institute Media Madness for more than 15 years.

Thanks also go to Carol Copple, my editor at NAEYC for the original edition of this book *(Remote Control Childhood? Combating the Hazards of Media Culture)* and to Holly Bohart and Kathy Charner, my NAEYC editors for the current edition, for all the time, thought, and energy they have given to this project.

And last but not least, deep thanks and appreciation go to my dear family: my husband, Gary Goldstein; my son, Eli Levin-Goldstein; and Eli's wife, Andrea Lubrano, all of whom have always valued and supported my work; and to my 98-year-old father, Arthur, who has followed and cared about my work from the start.

Contents

Part Two: Helping Children Get Beyond Remote-Controlled Childhood in Classroom Settings

Preface

In the mid-1980s, many teachers with whom I worked became puzzled and concerned about the changes they were noticing in children's war play in the classroom. They found it harder to limit and redirect play with violent themes, especially among boys, than they had in the past. Children continued to engage in the play when the adults turned their attention elsewhere, and some boys seemed almost obsessed with the play. Teachers also found it harder to get girls and boys to play together than they had before (Levin & Carlsson-Paige 2006; Linn 2004).

What could explain the changes these teachers were seeing? After investigating, I was startled to discover that about a year before I started hearing teachers' concerns, there had been sudden and dramatic changes in childhood media and media culture that seemed to have gone almost unnoticed.

In 1984, the United States government deregulated marketing to children (Levin & Carlsson-Paige 2006; Linn 2004). First, by an act of Congress, the Federal Trade Commission (FTC) lost its power to regulate marketing to children and was allowed only to make recommendations to marketers. In addition, and more central to the concerns being voiced by teachers, the Federal Communications Commission (FCC) stopped setting rules for how children's television programming could be used to market products to children. For the first time it was possible for companies to market products to children through television programs.

After deregulation, many highly successful children's television programs emerged that targeted just boys or just girls. Those directed at boys often had violent themes: *Masters of the Universe, G.I. Joe, Teenage Mutant Ninja Turtles,* and *Mighty Morphin Power Rangers.* Shows such as *My Little Pony* and *Care Bears* were primarily directed at girls. Extreme gender divisions in commercial children's television programming became the norm.

In addition, deregulation of children's television brought about the proliferation of shows that were often called "program-length commercials." These programs highlighted products for children that were linked to almost everything children saw on the shows. This very quickly led to the licensing of thousands of media-linked products, a change that affected most aspects of children's lives—including the kinds of toys they wanted (often direct replicas of what they saw on the screen), the clothes they wore, and the food they ate. Toy manufacturers sold billions of dollars' worth of media-related products to families with young children. Children quickly learned—often from how these products were marketed to them—to ask for and even nag their parents to buy as many as possible. Since deregulation, many of the bestselling toys each year have been linked to media (Levin & Carlsson-Paige 2006; Linn 2004).

Since that time, media-linked marketing has branched out far beyond television programming (see, for example, Holt et al. 2007). Products are often marketed to children through media cross-feeding, in which television shows, movies, websites directed at children, video games, comic books, children's books, and—most recently—apps are all linked. Through media cross-feeding, many children are deluged with media messages and images throughout their day.

I have seen these changes, coupled with the rapid expansion of screen technology in the lives of children, present challenges for both teaching and parenting. Many teachers and parents I have interviewed through the years voice an increasing array of concerns about how popular media culture is affecting children. They see negative effects on children's play, language, social interactions, and gender roles. They report that when children play, instead of using what they know to create their own characters and scenarios, they act out a script from a television program, a movie, or a video game. This behavior points to the impact of the media, and products marketed through the media, on children. Many parents have told me that even when they managed to avoid buying a toy they felt was inappropriate, their children played with the banned product at other children's houses or even convinced their friends or other family members to give them the coveted toy as a birthday present.

These changes in marketing to children through media, coupled with the explosion in children's interaction with various forms of media, have helped me better understand the concerns I was hearing and continue to hear from teachers and, increasingly, parents. These concerns are what led me to coin the term *remote-controlled childhood* for the first edition of this book. That is, I realized that *more and more of children's attitudes, values, interests, and behavior run the risk of being controlled by their experiences with the popular media culture and by their use of and expose to screens instead of being actively formed and created by children themselves.* Even more important, I realized that the media can control not just *what* lessons children learn, but also *how* they learn, or process, these lessons.

This concept of remote-controlled childhood is more relevant today than ever. It has become central to my understanding of how children are growing up in the ever-expanding media age. It has led me to conclude that, as early childhood educators, we need to make a commitment to better understand how media culture is affecting children and families and to find effective ways to help children get *beyond remote-controlled childhood.* And this is what I hope this book will help us do.

Taming the Media in Young Children's Lives

Since I wrote the first edition of this book, titled *Remote Control Childhood? Combating the Hazards of Media Culture* (Levin 1998), the influence of media and media culture on young children's lives has continued to grow to an almost unimaginable degree. From birth, today's children are growing up in an environment that is saturated with media culture—on screens such as television, movies, computers, tablets, MP3 players, eReaders, smartphones, and more almost every day, as well as all the products that are linked to what children see on screens.

Media culture forms an increasingly central part of children's experience and affects the very foundation children use to build an understanding of their world, how it works, and how they fit into it. And as it does, media culture influences how children behave and treat one another. It also shapes *how* they learn, *what* they learn, what they *want* to learn—and much more.

It behooves us, as early childhood professionals, to understand the power of media in children's lives—and how it has changed childhood—for the better as well as for the worse. Many long-established early childhood practices may not be the best approaches for working with and teaching children growing up in today's world. Many of the earlier approaches may not adequately take into account the power that media culture has and can have in shaping children and their learning.

The more we understand how today's media environment influences children's development, learning, behavior, relationships, and ideas about the world, the better equipped we will be to build on the positive aspects of media culture in children's lives and to counteract the negative ones. And the better able we will be to shape appropriate educational and societal practices and policies.

Media: Communication channels through which content is delivered, including television programs, video games, movies, music, websites, advertisements, and apps.

Media culture: Consumer-oriented messages communicated through mass media, such as television programs, video games, movies, music, websites, apps, and advertisements. Media culture defines, targets, and then sells products to users. It shapes individuals' attitudes, values, behaviors, and skills.

Screen media: Content delivered by technology that has a screen, including that viewed on televisions, computers, smartphones, tablets, eReaders, and video game consoles.

Technology: The tools, devices, and other machines or equipment that deliver media, including televisions, computers, smartphones, radios, MP3 players, video game consoles, eReaders, and tablets.

However, few early childhood professionals have been trained to understand how the growth of media and technology in society affects young children, much less to know how to adapt educational practices to take those effects into account. Few teacher preparation programs address issues related to media culture in a meaningful or comprehensive way. Even if they did, things change so fast that it is hard to keep up with what we should know and can do. And if this is difficult for us, imagine the challenges for parents, who have to make decisions every day about the media in their children's lives.

It is my hope that *Beyond Remote-Controlled Childhood* will help you develop the framework you need to work effectively with children growing up in today's world—to get beyond the negatives and promote the positives for all of the children with whom you work. I hope it will also enable you to help their families to do so as well.

An Ongoing Journey to Build Understanding

In the introduction to the first edition of this book, I explained that even though I had been a developmental psychologist and an early childhood educator for a long time, it was my experiences raising a son in the escalating media culture of the 1980s and '90s that helped me understand how children were being affected by this escalation. That is when I coined the term *remote-controlled childhood* to describe what I saw happening: children's attitudes, values, interests, and behavior being controlled by the popular media culture they experience with screens instead of being actively formed and created by children themselves and the adults in their lives. My parenting experiences also helped me develop a framework for understanding and effectively dealing with this phenomenon that still deeply informs the content of this book.

My Firsthand Experience With the Intrusion of Media Culture

Soon after my son, Eli, entered kindergarten, he was invited to the birthday party of one of his new school friends. Calvin was a first-grader in his kindergarten–first grade classroom. I was a bit anxious because I had met his parents only once. Eli and I went shopping to buy Calvin a gift. After much discussion about what Calvin might like, Eli decided on something that was one of his favorites at the time—a fancy box of "smelling" magic markers (each color had a different smell) and a sketchpad.

When we arrived at the party, Eli happily ran off and after a brief chat with Calvin's parents, I left. When I returned at pickup time, Eli came bouncing up to me and enthusiastically asked me to "come see Calvin's gifts." What I saw was a pile of action figures and other items that were almost all connected to a television program or movie with "fighting" themes—*Masters of the Universe, G.I. Joe,* and *Transformers* had become very popular at that time. Over to the side sat the box of magic markers and sketchpad.

Calvin's mother came over to say hello. Trying to find a nonthreatening way to get a sense of her reaction to the gifts, I casually said, "It looks like

Calvin got an arsenal for his birthday." She shrugged and said, "We didn't allow any war toys into the house until Calvin's birthday party last year after he entered kindergarten. Several kids brought presents like this. I couldn't send them all back, so after that we had to change our approach. Then Calvin began nagging to see the TV shows that went with the toys. He had only watched at other houses until then."

Eli and I left the party. As we got into the car, I knew that the next time he was invited to a birthday party, there would be a lot more stress over what gift to buy. I also knew that the equilibrium we currently had reached over Eli's own toys would probably soon need to be renegotiated, especially as his own birthday party approached. I was right on both counts!

About a month later, Eli was at the next birthday party of a new school friend. When I went to pick him up, I found all the children huddled in a little room watching *Raiders of the Lost Ark*. It is a movie I would not have chosen for him to see at his level of development and experience because it contains scary and violent content that cannot possibly be understood by 5- and 6-year-olds. Once again, media had entered Eli's life in a way over which I had little control.

The next school year, first grade, began with the Teenage Mutant Ninja Turtles as a major presence in the play culture of Eli and his friends. The television show and toys had rapidly become enormously popular, but there wasn't yet a movie. Eli had seen the show on television a few times, always with an adult present. Then, the night before the movie was due to open, he received a call from the child in his class who was the "turtle expert," inviting him to go to the opening after school on Friday. Eli was thrilled to have been chosen to accompany the class expert to the opening. Fortunately (I thought), we were going out of town after school on Friday, so to Eli's great unhappiness and disappointment, we had to turn down the invitation. But when I took Eli to school on Monday morning, he and I quickly realized that he was the only boy in his classroom who had not seen the movie. I knew the issue of his seeing the movie was far from over.

A couple of years later, we were on an airplane that aired an action movie on the big screen with a rape scene that showed all but the actual sex act (according to the airlines, it was "edited for family viewing"). Even without headphones, Eli *saw* his first rape. I expressed my concern to the flight attendant about the inappropriateness of the movie for children and asked how I could voice a complaint. Several other parents on the plane overhead what I said and expressed their thanks.

Soon after the airplane episode, the well-known boxer Mike Tyson went on trial for rape. The coverage of the trial was everywhere in the news. While we rarely watched the news at our house when Eli was around, he arrived home from school one day to ask what rape was and whether I had heard about Mike Tyson. While I was glad that Eli felt he could come to me with his questions about what he had seen and heard, I realized that more was at issue than entertainment media; many children were also affected by what they heard about in the news.

Throughout Eli's childhood, my husband, Gary Goldstein, and I struggled to create a home where media was consumed responsibly and thoughtfully. We always tried to achieve a balance between our own sense of what was appropriate from our adult perspective and Eli's interests, desires, and experiences.

But despite our best efforts as parents, we watched media enter our son's life in ways over which we felt we had little or no control, and it became an increasingly powerful influence on him. Most of the time Gary and I felt like we were holding our fingers in a hole in the dike, and even though water kept trickling in, we needed to keep our fingers there to prevent a flood. Sometimes we felt that media was taking control of our son—that he was becoming *remote controlled* by the media in his life. In the process of trying to stem the flood, we learned a lot about how to help him understand media and navigate its ever-changing currents. Sometimes the parents of Eli's friends shared our concerns; sometimes we had to work things out with parents who thought it was all mostly okay. This created an ongoing set of issues for us.

My experiences with Eli have kept me forever empathic toward parents and professionals in their efforts to deal with media culture, and most likely forever committed to continuing to be so. I have worked with many, many parents since the first edition of this book who say they have gone through some version of what I have described. Gary and I were fortunate because of the education and resources we had available to help us address our media concerns. Many parents struggle to meet their families' basic needs and do not have the resources I did to try to keep my finger in the dike.

Most families, like ours, face media issues in isolation, with few existing supports among other parents or from schools or the wider community. My son's school did not view media issues as something the school was responsible for addressing, nor did most of the schools I visited in those days. Few schools in the United States see this as their responsibility even today, although legislation to mandate comprehensive media literacy curriculum in kindergarten through grade 12 has been introduced in at least one state, Massachusetts (Massachusetts Media Literacy Consortium 2013). (Most other industrialized countries, however, include media literacy programs as a required part of their school curricula.)

My experiences parenting in the growing world of media culture would probably have been much easier and more effective if parents and teachers in my son's school community had worked together in their efforts to address family media issues, concerns, and struggles. Then, for example, there would have been an avenue for parents who had concerns to discuss gifts that were given at birthday parties or the movies their children watched at other families' houses. (To the school's credit, it eventually did do more than most schools I know to work on media literacy throughout the school community. And what they did has contributed to the content of this book.)

It would have been even more helpful if parents, schools, and communities all over the country were also working together on media issues. Then I might not have felt like the first parent ever to complain about a rape being shown during an airplane movie when many children were on board. And if the airlines had received a deluge of complaints from parents about the films they showed on board, they might have given more consideration to the needs of children when deciding which movies to air. We would have had the combined power of us all—a whole village—to counteract the problems created by the media for our children and to work together for the good of all children.

It was my awareness that those in schools and other professional settings were failing to help children and families address media and to incorporate messages about media into their work with children that led me to write the first edition of *Remote Control Childhood*. I deeply believed then, as I do now, that to fully meet our responsibilities as early childhood professionals, we need to understand how media culture is affecting children and to learn to use this knowledge to adapt how we work with children in the media age. I hoped that *Remote Control Childhood* would help early childhood professionals do this.

As I began the daunting task of revising *Remote Control Childhood* more than a decade after the first edition was published, Eli turned 30. I can see where Gary's and my efforts to address the media culture when he was a child have led. I feel a lot of satisfaction at what we were able to accomplish, but I am also humbled by what we could not do. What we dealt with is in many ways the tip of the iceberg compared with the effects of media culture and technology in the lives of today's children. The nature and scale of what is happening today makes my job as a parent then seem much less complicated than it would be if I were raising Eli today.

The issues have become more important and more complex. Even as there is a growing trend, often unsupported by research, to integrate technology into more and more aspects of early childhood classroom life, there is cause for concern over early screen use. The American Academy of Pediatrics (AAP) (American Academy of Pediatrics, American Public Health Association, & National Resource Center for Health and Safety in Child Care and Early Education 2011), for example, has recommended no screens for children under age 2 and no more than two hours a day of screen time for older children (no distinction is made between home and school; it is about *total* screen time). In addition, along with several other early childhood organizations, the AAP has recommended no more than half an hour per week of screen time for children over age 2 in early care and education settings.

I have been working with a growing village of parents and educators all over the world. Their experiences (and struggles) with media culture and their efforts to develop appropriate ways to respond have been a key source of my growing understanding of the issues. Their efforts and questions have inspired me to continue this work. And my parenting experiences keep me as committed as ever to helping early childhood professionals make *informed decisions* and *work together* to address the impact of today's ever-expanding screen and media culture on children and to help them develop their full potentials—socially, emotionally, physically, and intellectually.

We need to understand how media culture is affecting children and to use this knowledge to adapt how we work with children.

I am writing *Beyond Remote-Controlled Childhood* to help to further build the village that *Remote Control Childhood* began. I hope it will contribute to a new wave of activism and collaboration that will help children navigate today's media age and create the most positive media climate for children that we can—one in which adults, and adults and children, are working together rather than apart to make good media decisions. A little bit of effort from each of us along the lines of the discussions, activities, and actions suggested in this book will go a long way toward helping to grow that village. And through our efforts we can work in homes, schools, and communities, and with policy makers, television stations, and the media industry to make media decisions based on the best interests of our children.

What *Beyond Remote-Controlled Childhood* Does and Does Not Do

The media culture that is delivered to children through more and more forms of technology continues to grow and change with breathtaking speed. Often the innovations make questionable claims about the benefits they provide children. Many adults feel it is important to understand all the options, so they are prepared to choose the most current and "best" ones at home or at school. And while keeping up on technology and media can be helpful, it is *not* the purpose of this book.

When you finish reading *Beyond Remote-Controlled Childhood,* I hope you will have the knowledge and tools you need to make informed, effective decisions about the media in children's lives and how to address it. However, you will *not* be an expert on everything that is out there, because due to the speed with which things change, your knowledge would be out of date almost immediately. This book also aims to help you apply key issues about media in children's lives to *all* media—for example, the impact of being involved with a screen instead of with the real world is relevant for all media, as is how children's level of thinking affects the meaning they derive from what they experience on a screen. Having a broad knowledge base about the underlying issues and how to address them provides an essential framework for making good media choices and for dealing comprehensively with the range of ways that ever-changing media and technology are affecting childhood.

Throughout the book, I have included many stories that teachers and parents have shared with me about media-related experiences they have had with children. I have used the more dramatic ones because they clearly illustrate the issues being addressed. Furthermore, they tend to be the kinds of stories that teachers and parents have brought to me when asking for help to understand what is going on and how to address it. But they do not necessarily illustrate the only or even the most typical way that the particular issue being addressed comes up. Although media can certainly provide many positive experiences for children, and I believe adults can and should help children capitalize on these, the focus of this book is primarily on the negative impact of media and technology.

How *Beyond Remote-Controlled Childhood* Is Organized

This book is divided into three parts. Part One ("Establishing a Foundation for Action") focuses on background information that will help you build the foundation you need to understand media and media culture and how to address their negative effects on children. Part Two ("Helping Children Get Beyond Remote-Controlled Childhood in Classroom Settings") provides information about developing strategies for working effectively with children in classrooms to address the many ways media is a part of their lives. Finally, Part Three ("Working Outside the Classroom to Help Children Get Beyond Remote-Controlled Childhood") focuses on strategies for handling media issues outside the classroom—with parents, in schools, and in the wider community.

Throughout the book, you will find information that explains the important points underlying each media-related issue. You will also find guidelines to help you clarify how to work on these issues, action ideas that provide concrete suggestions for how you might begin, and numerous examples that illustrate how teachers, parents, and others working on these issues have translated the suggestions here into practice in their particular settings.

What you will not find are simple prescriptions about what to do to solve all the problems you may be facing. Complex problems require complex and ever-evolving solutions; the more you can shape your use of the contents of this book to fit your situation, the more effective and meaningful your efforts will be. Use this book in a way that works for you. Start small, adapt the suggestions here, build on them, see how things go. Share your efforts and successes with others.

This book is written to help teachers as they work with children today, as well as to help teachers work closely with families around these issues. Some sections may seem more relevant to your situation and needs than others. But you will find information in all the chapters that can be adapted for both school and home and that will also help teachers and parents better understand each other's points of view.

Thank you for finding ways—both big and small—to create the village we need to protect children from the hazards of media culture, to counteract the harm that it can cause, and to promote the positive aspects of technology, media, and the media culture in children's lives.

Activism and collaboration will help us create the most positive media climate for children that we can.

Establishing a Foundation for Action

PART ONE

Remote-Controlled Childhood: An Overview

Remote-Controlled Childhood: An Overview

Four-year-old Mandy's mother has washed Mandy's beloved princess lunch box. Mandy arrives at school with her lunch in a generic plastic bag because the lunch box didn't dry in time to pack her lunch. Mandy begins to sob when the other girls tell her she won't be able to sit at the usual "princess table" for lunch—"It's only for girls with princess lunch boxes!"

* * *

Six-year-old Jason's teacher asks him what books he likes to read at home. He excitedly explains, "I don't have to read books at home. My computer reads them to me!"

* * *

Kindergartner Melanie is sitting next to her teacher in the school cafeteria on the first day of school. She points to a nearby table and tells her teacher, "Those are the popular girls." Surprised, the teacher asks her, "How do you know?" Melanie replies, "They have the 'right' clothes. I saw it on TV." Then she sadly adds, "My mom won't buy me those. They cost too much."

* * *

Seven-year-old Daryn has been having nightmares, waking up at night and not being able to go back to sleep. After much reluctance, he tells his parents that his 11-year-old cousin showed him the video game Grand Theft Auto when he visited him the previous week. Looking worried, Daryn says he promised his cousin he wouldn't tell anyone. (Grand Theft Auto is rated M for mature audiences, in part because of the violence depicted.)

The environment in which many young children are growing up today is saturated with screen media such as television programs, movies, apps, video and computer games, and Internet websites. Children have a rapidly expanding number of ways to access this screen media—including through televisions, computers, and handheld devices such as tablets, smartphones, and video game consoles. In addition, children are exposed to numerous toys

Media: Communication channels through which content is delivered, including television programs, video games, movies, music, websites, advertisements, and apps.

Media culture: Consumer-oriented messages communicated through mass media, such as television programs, video games, movies, music, websites, apps, and advertisements. Media culture defines, targets, and then sells products to users. It shapes individuals' attitudes, values, behaviors, and skills.

Screen media: Content delivered by technology that has a screen, including that viewed on televisions, computers, smartphones, tablets, eReaders, and video game consoles.

Technology: The tools, devices, and other machines or equipment that deliver media, including televisions, computers, smartphones, radios, MP3 players, video game consoles, eReaders, and tablets.

and products that are linked to what they see on screens. This media-saturated environment touches most aspects of children's lives and is a central part of the foundation they are building to understand their world, how it works, how they fit into it, and how they can influence it. Often it affects how they behave and treat one another. It even shapes how they learn, what they want to learn—and much more (see, for example, Lillard & Peterson 2011 and Pagani et al. 2010, both listed in the Resources section of this book).

Not all media exposure and technology use is inherently negative or passive. There can be situations where children use technology to write, create, learn, and share information. Video-chatting with a grandparent who lives far away can be a meaningful way to keep in touch. In addition, not all young children are exposed to the same types and amounts of screen use. Nevertheless, the ever-growing influence of media exposure and technology use means that adults should be knowledgeable about and pay close attention to children's screen-related activities. What children are experiencing and learning through media can be cause for concern. The previous examples illustrate the kinds of stories I hear regularly from teachers and parents about how the influence of media and technology on children surfaces at school and home, affecting children's thinking, behavior, interests, and relationships.

Growing Up in Today's Media-Saturated World

While not all media use results in predictable outcomes, and we need much more research that systematically documents media's effects, the previous examples make it clear that as educators who work to promote young children's well-being, we must learn more about the impact of media use and how to respond effectively to children in situations like those described. As Principle 1.1 of the NAEYC Code of Ethical Conduct states, "Above all, we shall not harm children" (NAEYC 2011, 3). We need to take seriously our role and responsibility in understanding what children are exposed to, how it is affecting them, and what we can do to promote optimal development and learning in today's media culture. Part Two of this book will give you many practical ideas and strategies for doing this, but first, let's take a look at some of the issues surrounding the influence of media and technology on many children's lives.

Ever since the 1950s when television became a regular feature in family life, its influence on children has been the subject of study and debate. With each new type of screen device offered to consumers, both our understanding of and our differing opinions about its impact on children have continued to grow. At least in part because of the quickly changing technology landscape, the research that is needed to understand the impact of each new product always trails far behind the assimi-

---

Box 1.1

US Supreme Court: No Regulations on the Sale of Violent Video Games to Children

On June 6, 2011, the US Supreme Court struck down, on First Amendment grounds, a California law that banned the sale and rental of violent video games to children (Liptak 2011). While such a law would not have prevented older children and adults from showing such games to younger children, it would have provided a strong statement about society's role and responsibility in protecting young children from media violence.

lation of the product into children's lives. Unlike other government efforts to protect children from the release and marketing of potentially harmful products, such as alcohol, there is inadequate regulation and oversight governing the release of new technology devices that might affect the lives of children.

Media in the Lives of Children
Connected Children

Many children today are growing up in an environment connected to media and media culture in many aspects of their lives, often beginning soon after birth. Despite the American Academy of Pediatrics' (AAP) recommendation of no screen time for children younger than 2 years old and less than two hours a day for older children, 40 percent of 3-month-old infants are regular viewers of screen media (Zimmerman, Christakis, & Meltzoff 2007). This percentage has likely increased since that survey was done. Thirty percent of infants one year and younger have a television in their bedroom, and children younger than 2 who watch television spend twice as much time watching television and videos as they do reading books (Rideout 2011). Technology-related products for these very young children continue to proliferate, in part because the often unsubstantiated claims of manufacturers lead many parents to believe that such products are beneficial for their children's development (see, for example, Campaign for a Commercial-Free Childhood 2012a in the Resources section). My most recent find, just as this book goes to press, is a potty seat with a built-in stand for an iPad for the child to use to work on all sorts of skills while sitting on the potty (Crisp 2013). Yet there is growing evidence of the negative effects of screen use at such a young age (see Box 1.4 on page 17).

Television remains the most consumed technology among young children, especially among children from families with low incomes, although newer forms are prevalent as well (Gutnick et al. 2011). As children age, the amount of time they spend with screen media increases, although the results of studies do not always agree on how much time children are connected to screens. One study found that children ages 2 to 4 years average more than two hours a day with screens (Rideout 2011). Other research found that children ages 2 to 5 years spend more than 32 hours a week using a screen (McDonough 2009). For many children, this is more time than they spend in any other activity except sleeping. It can be more time than they spend in school settings. Research shows that screen time may be habit forming: The more time young children engage with screens, the more dependent on screens they can become and, as they get older, the more they tend to protest having to turn off the devices, (Christakis & Zimmerman 2006).

Dealing with the effects of media is not just a family responsibility. Early childhood educators also have an important role to play. As you begin to use

> For a detailed description of existing media regulations and their limitations, see Jordan 2008. Campaign for a Commercial-Free Childhood (www.commercial freechildhood.org) details numerous examples of the failure of government agencies to create and enforce regulations that protect children from media-related issues.

Box 1.2

Media and Minority Children

In 2011, Northwestern University's Center on Media and Human Development released a report documenting how media and technology play a greater role in the lives of children from minority families (Rideout, Lauricella, & Wartella). Two findings from the report are that children from minority families are more likely to 1) live in homes where the television is always on and 2) eat in front of the television.

the information in this book to engage with families around the topic of media and technology, you can support parents in their efforts to understand how media may be influencing their children and to encourage other activities at home. Realize, too, that there are many activities that parents and children can share with each other, and that you can help them with this. When parents and children interact, with or without technology, parents gain a better sense of what their children are learning and how they can influence that learning.

What Connected Children See on Screens

While not all the content children see on a screen is worrisome, much of it is cause for concern. For example, there are many stereotyped images about gender, race, and class in the media that children see. Television shows and movies, in particular, communicate many messages about how people should look, how they treat one another, and how they solve their conflicts (see, for example, Children Now 2012; Linn & Poussaint 1999; and Sun & Picker 2001, all listed in the Resources section). These portrayals often do not accurately reflect what many adults want children to imitate and learn.

Take a look, too, at media violence. By the age of 18, the typical American child will view more than 200,000 acts of violence on television, including more than 16,000 murders. Children's television programming, particularly cartoons, contains up to 20 violent acts an hour (Beresin 2010). Most of that violence occurs on programs that were created to "entertain."

Violent content also appears in other kinds of media, such as computer video games, which can be viewed on game consoles, computers, smartphones, tablets, and notebooks. According to Reuters ("Factbox" 2011), the global market for video games alone is valued at $65 billion. A large proportion of video games, especially the bestsellers, are violent, and the violence is increasingly graphic and realistic. When children are actively "participating" in violence by playing such video games, the negative impact on children can be greater than the impact of passively viewing violence on the screen (Anderson 2003). With the 2011 Supreme Court ruling that legislation cannot ban the marketing of such games to children (Liptak 2011)—even if they are rated for much older children or adults— it becomes harder for parents to protect children from exposure to video game violence, particularly as the games become ever more prevalent in the peer culture of slightly older children. Many kindergarten and first grade teachers tell me that they are concerned about the kinds of violent video games they hear children talking about. Parents also tell me that when their children go to the homes of friends who have siblings a few years older, their young children are exposed to video games that have violent themes or are inappropriate for young children in other ways.

In addition to violence in entertainment media, many children see and hear about real violence from news reports in the media. Many reports are broadcast over the radio when children are riding in the car or are televised at dinnertime when many families who eat together do so with their televisions on. And when events happen such as the December 2012 elementary school

When parents and children interact, with or without technology, parents gain a better sense of what their children are learning.

shooting tragedy in Newtown, Connecticut, even parents who are very protective of what their children see on the news say they feel quite helpless in protecting their children from exposure to it.

There is also an enormous amount of marketing to children through the media. According to a 2007 report by the FTC, children ages 2 to 11 see more than 25,000 advertisements a year on television alone (Holt et al.). This figure does not include the rapid increase in advertising through other media sources, such as the Internet; apps on smartphones, tablets, and computers; video games; and even school buses and schools (Campaign for a Commercial-Free Childhood 2013b; Levin & Asquith 2013). Nine states, for example, allow advertisements on the exterior of school buses; others allow them inside buses (Campaign for a Commercial-Free Childhood 2013b).

Also missing from this figure are the thousands of toys and other products that are linked to children's television programs, movies, and other media. Almost every major media program for children has a line of licensed merchandise, including food, toys, clothing, and accessories. This is true even for most of the programming on public television. In the first half of 2012, media-licensed toys accounted for 27 percent of the toy industry's approximately $21.2 billion in annual sales (Toy Industry Association 2012, 2013). And while toy sales figures have remained relatively flat or fallen slightly (Zimmerman 2012), many traditional toys, such as blocks, LEGOs, and Play-Doh, now have links to media. For instance, as I am writing this, the websites of national toy stores list construction toys that are linked to many of the most popular television programs and movies.

A report from the Kaiser Family Foundation (2007) states that the food and beverage industry spends $2 billion annually to market foods to children, even as concerns about childhood obesity continue to grow. Children will see almost 4,000 food ads each year, many of which are on television. Eighty-one percent of the food ads children see are for candy, sugar-coated cereals, fast food, or soft drinks. These foods have been linked to rising levels of poor nutrition and higher levels of childhood obesity (Harris et al. 2009). (For more information on food marketing to children, see Campaign for a Commercial-Free Childhood 2012b and Center for Science in the Public Interest 2012, both listed in the Resources section.)

For more facts and figures about marketing to children, including the marketing of media-linked toys, scan this QR code or go to the website of the Campaign for a Commercial-Free Childhood (www.commercialfree childhood.org/resources-factsheets).

ACTION IDEA   Box 1.3

The Impact of Media on Children

Information

• Copy the information in Box 1.4 on page 17 and share it with others.

• Add new and updated research facts that you read or hear about in the news.

Reflection Questions

• How are the children in my class affected by the media in their lives?

• What do the children in my class and their families think about how media affects their lives?

• What is the best way to offer families the information I have learned about how media affects children?

Suggested Strategies or Interactions With Children and Families

• Conduct a class meeting with the children about what you have noticed in their play.

• At a parent meeting, copy and distribute the information in Box 1.4 to the families, and lead a discussion about media and children. Objectively describe the children's play in the classroom. Share information and strategies with families that they can use to address this issue. (See Chapter 10 for more information about possible strategies.)

As we will discuss in Part Two, teachers and parents can do several things to counteract the violent and stereotyped content children are often exposed to through media. (Some initial suggestions are offered in Box 1.3 on page 15. These suggestions and others will be explored more fully in Parts Two and Three of this book.)

Screens, Screens Everywhere

Screens are entering into more and more of the basic activities of childhood, both in and out of the home. In addition to seeing a wide range of content on television screens in public spaces such as restaurants, shopping malls, airports, and airplanes, many children now use handheld devices—some designed specifically for children, some intended for adults. The content that children can use on these devices includes applications that claim to teach the alphabet and much more, movies that can be downloaded at any time, and games to play through online virtual communities designed specifically for children and often linked to television programs, movies, and toys.

Increasingly, at restaurants, in airports, or even when walking down the street, I see family members of all ages engaged with their own individual screens instead of talking with each other. This behavior reduces the time children spend interacting with other people and with real things in the real world. When looking at the impact of media and screens in children's lives, we need to consider the typical activities that children used to do that they now do less often or not at all. And we need to ask *how* changes in the way children spend their time affect their development and learning and, therefore, how we should take this information into account in our work with them.

Finally, when children do turn off their screens and play, often their toys are linked to specific media. That is, toys are direct replicas of what children have seen on a screen; are electronic, with buttons to push or flashing lights; or come with a special code to give children access to a website. So even when children are disconnected from screen devices, such toys can keep them connected to their screen-time experiences and to the secondhand content that other people have created for them. This offers one more example of how screens can contribute to remote-controlled learning and play.

The Effects of Being Connected to Media (And Disconnected From Direct Experience)

After a week of school vacation, a teacher held a group meeting with the 6- and 7-year-old children in her class. When she asked them to share their favorite activity from their vacation, all the children gave a media example. For the boys, it was playing video games, often violent ones. For the girls, it was mostly viewing the current female performers popular with young girls. When the teacher asked the children what they would have done on vacation if they didn't have any screens to use, they stared at her blankly.

As mentioned, much of what media culture is teaching children is not what many of the adults who care about children would choose for them to learn, or what child development knowledge tells us children need for optimal development and learning. A growing body of research can help us understand how and why much media fails the test. On one hand, there are a few studies that look at programs designed to help children learn in developmentally appropriate ways, as well as entertain them. One of the first such studies looked at *Mister Rogers' Neighborhood*, a television show that stopped production in the early 2000s. The program was aimed primarily at children ages 2 to 5 to help them learn about themselves and the world around them. The study found that it did promote positive social behavior in children (Carnegie Corporation of New York 1996). At the time of this writing, a spinoff of *Mister Rogers' Neighborhood*, titled *Daniel Tiger's Neighborhood*, has debuted. While the new program is animated, the producers claim to be basing it on strategies, goals, and values similar to those of the original show.

On the other hand, there is a larger body of research showing that much of the screen media directed at children can undermine, or even harm, their development and behavior. In fact, what we now know about children's media use has led pediatrician Victor Strasburger to claim that "the media can have an impact on virtually every concern parents and pediatricians have about children and teenagers" (2009, 655). Box 1.4 summarizes key areas of concern.

For a discussion of research findings on children's television programs and promotion of early literacy, see Moses 2009, listed in the Resources section.

Shared Responsibility and a Call to Action

Too much of the responsibility for managing young children's screen time and addressing the effects of media, media violence, and the media culture on children is placed on parents. The media and toy industries, as well as many government officials, policy makers, and teachers, tell parents that if they would just set limits and say no to children's technology and screen use, there would not be a problem with it. But there are difficulties with this logic. When the US government deregulated marketing to children in 1984, companies could market products to children through television programs for the

Box 1.4

Research Highlights on the Effects of Media on Children

- The more time children use screens in the early years, the more they tend to protest turning them off when they are older (Christakis & Zimmerman 2006).
- Toddlers' use of screens has been connected to the following problems in later childhood: 1) lower math and school achievement, 2) reduced physical activity, and 3) higher levels of obesity.
- Screen time for children younger than 3 years old has been associated with irregular sleep patterns and delayed language acquisition.
- Increased screen exposure in early childhood has been connected with 1) higher levels of aggression, 2) sleep disturbances, 3) weight problems, and 4) shorter attention spans.
- Children who have two or more hours of screen time a day tend to exhibit more psychological difficulties, such as 1) hyperactivity, 2) emotional and behavior problems, and 3) difficulties with peers.
- Media violence can contribute to 1) aggressive behavior, 2) desensitization to violence, 3) nightmares, and 4) fear of being harmed (American Academy of Pediatrics 2009).
- The more time children spend with screens, the less time they spend engaged in creative play, which is a key foundation for later learning, constructive problem solving, and creativity.

Note: Unless otherwise noted, the facts in this box come from Campaign for a Commercial-Free Childhood 2012b.

first time. Over the years, the research I conducted showed that raising a "post-deregulation" child—after 1984—presented many challenges that parents raising "pre-deregulation" children did not have to face—related to both the content children were seeing on the screen and what and how they played when they turned off the screen. Since then, these challenges have only continued to escalate.

Today, many parents of young children are "first-generation deregulation parents." They were in their early childhood years when deregulation of children's television and marketing to children were occurring, which led to an environment increasingly influenced by screens—both watching screens and having products linked to screens. Many of today's teachers grew up in a similar environment. These parents and teachers are now raising or teaching "second-generation deregulation children," and having children deeply connected to screens and media culture can seem normal.

At the same time, I work with many parents of young children who say they can, and do, try very hard to take on the roles of protector and regulator. These parents regularly tell me that their efforts do make a difference. But many problems still arise—for example, continual struggles at home with their children nagging to see, or sneaking to see, content that the parents have banned. Many also say that they have tried to set clear limits on screen time. But screens have gradually crept into their children's lives more and more until the parents feel that screens have become a much too dominant force. In addition, despite their best efforts, they often meet with only limited success because their children are exposed to media programs and products outside the home—at the homes of friends and relatives, in supermarkets, in restaurants, and in shopping malls. Box 1.5 offers a look at one parent's experience with a child's unexpected media exposure, along with

Box 1.5

How a Teenage Star Snuck Into a 5-Year-Old's Life

What Happened

Out of the blue, Ashley, age 5, excitedly told her mother that she knew Hannah Montana. The mother asked her how she knew about her, as the mother had been careful to keep her from watching the show. Ashley said that Aidan, her 11-year-old brother, had watched it with her, but she added that it was "just for a sneak, Mommy. It's a secret!"

What Would You Do . . .

• If this happened in your family?

• If a child in your class told you about the secret?

• If a parent told you about this situation and asked you what he or she should do?

What the Mother Did

The mother kept her cool and asked Ashley what she thought of Hannah. She said she thought Hannah was very pretty but that she "wasn't very nice." Her mother asked, "What did Hannah do that wasn't nice?" and Ashley said, "She poured blue paint all over her friend, and that was really mean!" The mother said she, too, thought that pouring blue paint over someone wasn't very nice and told her that was one of the reasons why the family hadn't watched the program. She added that Aidan shouldn't have let her watch it and that it would be a good idea not to watch it anymore. Ashley agreed that she didn't think she should watch it—even though her friends Jessie and Karla did.

Think About It

• What is your reaction to how the mother handled the situation?

• Why do you think she responded this way?

• Is there anything you would add or do differently?

some questions for reflection. We desperately need more research, especially longitudinal research, on the impact of various parenting and teaching strategies for addressing media culture and technology.

Families and teachers are not the only ones struggling with the effects of media and commercial culture on children. As you will see in the chapters that follow, all of society is affected by the lack of an informed, research-based, positive media environment for children that supports the efforts of families and early childhood professionals to promote children's healthy development, learning, and behavior. The lessons children are learning (and not learning) from the environment created by today's media are played out every day in classrooms, schoolyards, homes, and the wider community—and create special challenges for everyone.

As debate continues over which aspects of media are appropriate or inappropriate for children and over who is responsible for helping children use screens wisely, children are growing up in an environment in which the adults who care for and teach them often struggle to make informed, effective decisions about the media in children's lives (Campaign for a Commercial-Free Childhood, Alliance for Childhood, & Teachers Resisting Unhealthy Children's Entertainment 2012). It is time to recognize that families' efforts to combat the media's influence are constantly being undermined. It is a job they cannot possibly do on their own. It is time for all those who care about children to put aside the debate about who is to blame for the influence of media and to take action.

It is my hope that *Beyond Remote-Controlled Childhood* will help you develop the framework and strategies needed to take action and work effectively with children growing up in today's world—to move beyond the negatives and promote the positives for all of the children with whom you work. This book will help you work with families and colleagues to

◆ Make informed decisions about the screen media in children's lives at home and at school

◆ Adapt classroom practice to take into account the realities of remote-controlled childhood—the experiences of today's connected children

◆ Counteract the potentially harmful impact media can have on both the process and content of children's development and learning

◆ Press for change in society to create a media environment that is more supportive of children's healthy development

This book will help you take action to move beyond the negatives and promote the positives for all children.

A Developmental Perspective on Remote-Controlled Childhood

During one family's breakfast, a report came on the radio about the bombing of another country by the United States. Suddenly 6-year-old Brian jumped up and said, "I sure hope we have the Power Rangers there to help!" His mother reminded Brian that the Power Rangers were only pretend. He responded, "I know. But they can take off their [Power Ranger] outfits and then go fight."

Immediately 4-year-old Rosemarie chimed in, "Yeah, and they better have the Megazords with them, too. They sure make the Power Rangers strong."

Both children began prancing around the kitchen pretending to karate chop each other like the Power Rangers do. As their parents asked them to stop, Rosemarie burst into tears when one of Brian's karate chops caught her arm.

Children use both media and real-life experiences to build ideas about the world through a slow *process* of construction. They do not passively absorb information and ideas. They transform what they see and hear into something that is uniquely meaningful to them. The new meanings they make build on what they have discovered from prior experience. Each child's thinking is unique—no two children will ever create meaning in quite the same way, even from the same experience.

Brian and Rosemarie illustrate this process in their conversation after they hear about the bombing attack on the radio. They use what they already know about fighting—in this case, the Mighty Morphin Power Rangers—to try to understand the information they have heard about the bombing. For instance, Rosemarie knows that pretend Megazords are the Power Rangers' most powerful weapon, so in any fighting that must be what is needed. Brian knows that the Power Rangers are strong and can always win, so he decides they are needed to fight with the good guys (in this case, US troops). The

Power Rangers' costumes must be what makes them pretend, but if they take the costumes off, Brian reasons, then they would be real. What is pretend and what is real has quite a different meaning for Brian and Rosemarie than it has for adults.

Even though the particular event described took place in the 1990s, this is still the kind of process children need to go through to make meaning of their experiences (even if it's not the meaning we adults expect them to make). As they do, they build new ideas that they draw on when trying to make sense of their next new experience. This meaning-making process provides a helpful way to think about how children learn new and more sophisticated ideas and skills. The information you can gain about what they are thinking and learning as they go through this process can guide how you work with children and talk to them about media-related situations. This information can also help you find ways to connect what you want them to learn to what they already know and, when necessary, help you counteract inaccurate lessons children may be learning.

How Young Children Think Affects the Meanings They Construct From Their Experiences

As Rosemarie and Brian try to make sense of what they have heard on the news about the fighting and bombing, they reveal several of the special characteristics of young children's thinking that differ from more mature thinking. These characteristics, which are based on Piaget's theory of cognitive development, affect how Rosemarie and Brian, like all young children, interpret and learn from their new experiences from both real life and screens:

◆ Young children tend to have a hard time **fully distinguishing between pretend and real.** They may use what they have learned about good guys and bad guys and about fighting and weapons from a fictional program to interpret something they hear about actual violence. The fact that 6-year-old Brian had often been told that the Power Rangers are really actors does not stop him from giving them "real" soldier status. Four-year-old Rosemarie seems even less able to distinguish between pretend and real when she assumes that all fighters are like the Power Rangers and need Megazords to fight.

◆ Young children typically **focus on the most dramatic and concrete aspects of the situation.** They do not address the more abstract concepts underlying it. Brian and Rosemarie gravitate to the fighting and weapons rather than to the issues surrounding the fighting or what caused it.

◆ Young children usually **do not make logical causal connections.** They do not link what is happening to *why* it is happening or to the possible consequences. As they focus on the action and excitement of the fighting, Rosemarie and Brian do not think about the causes of the conflict between two countries or the pain and suffering that might result from the attack reported in the news.

Many of the concepts discussed in this chapter about how children think and build ideas about the world come from the work of Jean Piaget. For a more detailed summary of Piaget's work, see Wadsworth 2003.

◆ Young children tend to **focus on only one aspect of the situation at a time.** Their thinking is more like a series of separate, static photographs than a movie with interrelated events. They do not think about the whole picture and how the events relate to one another. This helps explain why it can be so hard for children to piece together situations using logical causality.

◆ Young children most commonly **think in dichotomous categories.** In fights you either win *or* lose. Characters are all good *or* all bad; the Power Rangers are clearly "good," while those they are fighting are "bad." Furthermore, anything the good guy's side does seems to be unquestionably all right because he is good, and the bad guys' actions are always wrong because they themselves are bad.

Children often struggle to comprehend the sexualized and violent content they see and hear in the media (Brown, Lamb, & Tappan 2009; Levin & Kilbourne 2009). This may be because these messages can be very jarring and confusing to young children, but they can also be very dramatic and salient.

The conversation in Box 2.1 on page 24 provides an example of media content coming to the surface in children's play in one early childhood setting. It reveals how and what 5-year-old Henry thinks after watching an early *Star Wars* movie at home. His comments to his teacher illustrate many of the characteristics of young children's thinking as described above. Henry's comments also illustrate the unique ways a particular child constructs meaning from what he knows about the movie and how play itself can provide a powerful vehicle for making meaning out of what children see on screens. The follow-up questions the teacher asks both respect what Henry says and help Henry build connections between the isolated ideas and actions he is using in the play and his thinking about them.

The commentary that accompanies the dialogue between Henry and his teacher points out the characteristics of Henry's thinking and demonstrates how the teacher works with him to try to better understand his thinking and gently stretch some of the ideas he has developed. Children are often surprised when adults ask them questions as this teacher does, without judging what they do and say. As you read this conversation, think about experiences you have had with children's play that provided similar opportunities to gain insight about their understanding of media experiences.

> The information you gain about what children are thinking and learning can guide how you talk to them about media-related situations.

Use What You Know About Children's Thinking and Meaning Making

Use the following tips as you seek to understand the ideas and concepts children have constructed from their experiences with media.

◆ **Commit to a slow, complex, and ongoing process.** The ideas you talk about while helping children understand situations like those discussed will need to be revised as children develop and as their circumstances change. Brian's parents had already told him that the Power Rangers were

Box 2.1

Working It Out Together: A Discussion About Henry's Understanding of *Star Wars*

Dialogue	Commentary
Teacher: Tell me about what you're making with the LEGOs.	• Throughout, the teacher uses **open-ended questions** or nonjudgmental statements to explore Henry's thinking.
Henry: *Star Wars* spaceships with lasers.	• His response focuses on the **most salient and powerful** feature of the spaceship—the laser.
T: Who uses the spaceships? **H:** Han Solo and Chewbacca. **T:** What do they use the spaceships for?	• The teacher tries to get a conversation going to find out what he knows and thinks. Play is a perfect opportunity to do this.
H: To fly in space. They go on their own. [Each has a spaceship.]	• He focuses on **one salient aspect** of the movie—a spaceship for each character.
T: What do they do in their spaceships?	• The teacher's questions stay focused on **concrete actions,** not abstract ideas.
H: Shoot bad guys if the bad guys are coming right toward them.	• He uses **dichotomous categories** for good and bad guys.
T: What do they shoot?	• She explores his thinking without making a value judgment about the fighting.
H: Bullets.	• He focuses on **one thing**—shooting—not the **illogic** of lasers shooting bullets.
T: And then what happens?	• She uses an **open-ended question** to learn more about what he is thinking.
H: Then if a bullet hits them they blow up. These go back [pointing to movable LEGO flaps].	• He focuses on **the most salient, dramatic aspect** of the shooting—the "blowing up," not the loss of life.
T: What did the bad guys do to make the good guys shoot the bullets at them?	• She tries to get him to focus on the **causality**—what bad thing they did.
H: They have things that can shoot out and this is where they shoot out.	• He stays focused on the **concrete characteristics,** not the causality.
T: Why do the good guys need to shoot?	• She tries again to get him to focus on the underlying causes.
H: To blow up the bad guys because they are mean to the good guys and the bad guys want to kill the good guys.	• He uses **dichotomous and static thinking**—bad guys do bad things because they are "mean" and they "kill."
T: Do you know why they want to kill the good guys?	• She tries to get at underlying causality.
H: Because they're not on the good guys' team.	• He is still focusing on **one thing at a time (good and bad).** He adds "teams" to the dichotomous categories; "killing" is not connected to real-world meanings or effects.

Box 2.1 cont'd

Dialogue	Commentary
T: Oh, so there are two teams? A good guys' team and a bad guys' team?	• She reflects his thinking back to him to see if he goes further with it.
H: Yeah, and Darth Vader is on the dark side and Luke Skywalker is on the light side.	• He continues to focus exclusively on good and bad and uses **concrete, tangible information** to further define his **dichotomous categories.**
T: Is that how you can tell who is on what team, by the colors that they wear?	• She seeks clarification of his thinking.
H: Well, well, not, well . . . I know because my friend, Paul, told me. He has lot of *Star Wars* toys, and he told me the dark side, some of Darth Vader's slaves have white on but they're bad guys.	• This question has him a bit confused and gets him outside of his focus on fighting. He is trying to make sense of his friend's information but still focuses on concrete issues. There's also confusion about how bad and good guys can both wear white.

not real before he heard the news report about the bombing, yet he still believed that they should go to fight. When his mother pressed the point that the characters were only pretend, he took his thinking a step further by dealing with what he thought made them pretend—their costumes. But Brian still has a long way to go before he is able to sort out the fantasy and reality of television characters as adults can.

◆ **Embed what you do into children's everyday lives and experiences.** Because young children learn by doing, this practice will ensure that your lessons are powerful. Henry's teacher connected the *Star Wars* discussion to what Henry was actually doing with the LEGOs. This provided a meaningful focus to his discussion. A next step for the teacher might be to help him compare and contrast what he says the *Star Wars* characters do with what Henry does in his own life. For instance, she might say, "So what else do you like to do with LEGOs when you're not playing *Star Wars*?" or, "I wonder why the good guys and bad guys always have to shoot when they have a problem. Remember when you and Jesse were mad at each other? How did you solve that problem?"

◆ **Learn what children think about what they have seen and experienced on screens, and the unique meanings they have made.** This can help you understand and respect the cultural diversity and individual experiences of the children with whom you are working. The teacher's discussion with Henry about *Star Wars* offers an example of how to collect the kind of information you need to work with children in unique and respectful ways.

◆ **Encourage children to say what they think.** Few efforts will ever go exactly as you plan them, nor will they go the same way twice. What is important is that you try to use and build on children's ideas and that you come up with solutions and conclusions together. Henry's teacher did not know where

Box 2.2

"I Want My Daddy to Get Diabetes!"

Here is another example of how a child constructs unique meaning from an experience with media culture—this time, television marketing—that can lead to confusion and misunderstanding.

A teacher was rather stunned when Aaron, a 4-year-old in her class, blurted out that he wanted his father to get diabetes. And he said it in a very excited, pleased way.

The teacher explained to Aaron that his family tried to eat healthy food so no one would get diabetes. Aaron looked genuinely puzzled and said, "But I want my daddy to get diabetes. They're really good cakes and we could eat them!"

The teacher later learned from Aaron's father that Aaron had seen an ad on television for diabetes-related products, including "delicious" diabetic-friendly desserts—apparently called "diabetes" in his mind. The ads convinced him that he had to have those "diabetes"!

What Would You Do?

• What are your reactions to this situation?

• How do the ideas discussed in this chapter about how children think and learn help you understand what happened?

• What would you do and say to help clear up Aaron's misconception? How would you help Aaron and his father respond to what Aaron told you?

• What experiences have you had with young children that illustrate this kind of thinking and meaning making around media and technology issues?

ACTION IDEA

Box 2.3

How Children Understand the Media They See

When children bring media content into their play or conversations, try to learn more about it:

• Observe and take notes about the topics that come up—learn from whom, when, and how they got this information.

• Ask children open-ended questions to find out more about what they have seen on screens, how they understand it, and what they like about it.

• Keep learning. The more you learn, the better prepared you will be to address situations when they arise in the classroom.

---

her questions about *Star Wars* might lead, so she took her cues from his responses. She did this without making value judgments about fighting that might make him feel that it was not okay to say what he really thought.

◆ **Help children work out their own ideas that grow out of what they already know.** Ask questions or introduce ideas that might help counteract the inaccurate or even harmful lessons children may be learning. Brian's mother extended and complicated his thinking a little bit when she pointed out that the Power Rangers were not real. Brian dealt with her comment by saying the Power Rangers could take off their costumes. Henry's teacher's comments nudged him to begin to deal with the complexity of the color white not just being for the good guys. Avoid trying to get children to think as adults do by just giving them adult ideas about media in simpler words. Finding meaningful ways to connect what you want children to learn to what they already know can help bring about real change in their thinking and behavior.

Throughout this book you will find many other examples of teachers working to help children stretch their thinking about violence and sexual issues and much more.

Challenges to Responding Effectively

Brian and Rosemarie's parents made a conscientious effort to limit the amount of television their children watched, as well as their exposure to other media. While this is essential, *adults' efforts to protect children from exposure will rarely be enough*. Some media messages will continue to reach children because they permeate the environment—not just on screens but in children's daily lives outside the home. So children still need adult help to make sense of the media messages about violence and other subjects that they do encounter. Teachers have an essential role to play in minimizing the risk that children will learn negative lessons from these messages.

It is not enough to simply give children information about what they are seeing and hearing on screens. Because children actively make their own meanings and these meanings are generally different from the way adults understand an issue, children will interpret what you try to teach them in their own unique ways. Keep this in mind in your efforts to help children make sense of media content.

A Closer Look at Remote-Controlled Childhood: How Media Culture Affects Children

A Closer Look at Remote-Controlled Childhood: How Media Culture Affects Children

A teacher is showing 4-year-old Jason how to play a lotto game. As she does, he asks a few times with increasing animation, "Where's the shooting?" Finally she tells him, "There isn't any shooting in this game. You just use the cards." Looking puzzled, Jason responds: "Then how do you win if there's no shooting?" Jason does settle down with the teacher's help and begins to play the game with apparent interest.

As you can see from this account, children sometimes learn surprising lessons from screen media about the world and how it works. In fact, media is a teacher that often competes with us for children's minds and attention. Efforts to deal effectively with what children are learning when they use screens will need to take into account the scope of media culture's influence and power on children in general, as well as its effects on individual children. To understand the full impact of media culture and technology and to develop strategies that will help minimize their negative effects on children, I have found it very helpful to divide the issues surrounding children's screen use into two broad categories.

First, we need to look at the *content* lessons—what children learn from screen media. What they learn is very different from real-world, hands-on, direct experiences with real people and objects. Because media and the culture it communicates are everywhere—on television programs, video games, and apps for computers and tablets; in everyday places like grocery stores and restaurants; and on devices that are part of everyday life like smartphones and tablets—the world children live in is filled with media messages. Jason's assumption that fighting is what you do to win games illustrates some of the content he has learned from media.

The second category, which often receives less attention but is equally important, is how media and media culture affect the very way children learn—the *process* they use for interacting in the world and learning new concepts and skills. Chapter 2 explained that children construct meaning from their experiences; media culture can contribute to children becoming remote-controlled learners in the sense that they no longer strive to be active agents in control of their own learning but rather are programmed to imitate what they see on screens (Levin 1998). Jason also illustrates how media has influenced the process he uses to deal with his world—he has one strategy for playing a game: fighting.

As you will see in Part Two, which focuses on what teachers can do to counteract the effects of remote-controlled childhood, helping children learn to be in control of their own learning requires the use of teaching strategies that consider both content *and* process issues.

Content Issues: Media Culture Affects *What* Children Learn

Much of the criticism directed at children's media focuses on the content and its messages about who children are, how they should treat one another, what they should like and dislike, what it means to be a girl or a boy, and much more. Many of these messages are at cross-purposes with our aims as educators, making our jobs more difficult. While certainly not all media portray negative or stereotypical messages, those discussed in this chapter are prevalent in today's media culture.

Buying as the Source of Happiness

The onslaught of increasingly sophisticated marketing and media-linked products that followed the deregulation of marketing to children has become a major force in children's development and education. Young children, because of their thought processes (see Chapter 2), are especially vulnerable to exploitative marketing messages. For example, when young children see advertising or product-based programs, they focus on the most concrete aspects of what they see and do not put the product into a meaningful context (Levin 2009; Linn 2005).

With deregulation allowing products to be marketed directly to children through media in enticing ways, many children become obsessed with media-related products and try to get their parents to buy them. This pervasive marketing creates stress in many homes and competition among children in school over who has the latest, most coveted item. Fleeting happiness often comes from getting the coveted item, but when children find that the object does not live up to its promises, they often become bored with it. And there is always something newer and more desirable. This "I want it" cycle can cause children to focus their energy on getting the things they want more than on engaging in "I can do it" meaningful activities (Levin 2004). It can also help explain why some children often say they are bored in the midst of plenty.

Biased Messages About Gender, Race, and Socioeconomic Status

Children begin constructing ideas about similarities and differences among people very early in life. These ideas are built from what they see and hear about diversity in their immediate environment and in the wider society.

Today, many of children's ideas about gender, race, special needs, and economic and ethnic diversity come from indirect experience with news and entertainment media, toys, and popular culture, all of which can portray stereotypes (Levin 2003). In general, children see a majority of white characters portrayed (except for villains, who are often nonwhite), many more males than females, and more middle- and upper-class characters. The stereotypic messages children receive from screen media teach them about racial issues and what it means to be a member of a certain race, about what it means to be rich or poor and the role of consumerism, about what it means to be male or female, and about the nature of sexual relationships. And because of the way children think—focusing on one aspect at a time, for example—they are especially vulnerable to taking in stereotyped messages.

An important way children try to understand their gender identity is by looking at the world around them to see what girls and boys do. On screens, children see males and females portrayed in extremely different, gender-divided ways; for example, males are often shown as strong, powerful, and ready to fight, and females are often shown as focusing on having the right appearance. Children tend to focus on salient, concrete images that help them form dichotomous (contrasting) categories—that is, they look for the most graphic or extreme examples of differences between boys and girls to figure out what is and is not appropriate for their gender.

Mass media producers and marketers tend to use extreme gender divisions and stereotypes—violence for boys and sexualization and appearance for girls—as a marketing tool to capture boys' and girls' attention. When these highly stereotyped media messages defining gender are not offset by what children see and hear from others around them, they can develop narrow gender definitions for themselves, thereby restricting their opportunities to develop the full range of their potential (Levin & Kilbourne 2009; see also Martins & Harrison 2012 in the Resources section for a report about racial and gender differences in the relationship between children's television use and self-esteem).

Sexy Girls

Today even preschoolers are exposed to images of female sexy appearance, sexualized behavior, and unhealthily thin bodies in media and popular culture. On television, in videos, and at shopping malls, preschool girls see entertainers and cartoon characters wearing short skirts and belly button-exposing shirts.

Helping children learn to be in control of their own learning requires addressing both content *and* process issues.

They also see wedged-heeled shoes and makeup kits designed for children their age. Although they cannot fully understand what they see and hear, from a very young age they try to figure it out. As they do, media influences how they think about their bodies and about being female. According to the *British Journal of Psychology,* almost half of all girls ages 3 to 6 worry about being fat (Hayes & Tantleff-Dunn 2010). And a study published in *Pediatrics,* a journal of the American Academy of Pediatrics, found that eating disorders were on the rise among girls under age 12 (Rosen 2010). The media culture affects what children want to be, do, and wear. This exposure may cause some girls to see themselves and other girls as *objects,* judging one another by how they look and the clothes they wear. Some boys, too, learn to judge girls as objects.

Children are likely to bring this sexualized content into your classroom—for example, by performing sexy dances they see on television or wearing sexy clothes that inhibit their physical activity. In one particular classroom, after 5-year-old Jenna had an all-girls "High School Musical" birthday party, the girls began doing sexy "High School Musical" dances at school in the dramatic play area and at outdoor time. The teacher, in conjunction with her principal, decided to write parents a letter suggesting guidelines for age-appropriate birthday parties for girls (see Box 3.1).

When young girls see their gender portrayed in sexualized ways, their understanding of themselves as females and their social judgments can be heavily influenced by their perception of how they look, what they can buy, and their peers' self-perceptions (Dohnt & Tiggemann 2006). In addition, the model of the ideal female as portrayed in the media is one with a dangerously thin body, and even young girls can develop unhealthy relationships with their bodies in an effort to meet the ideal. Parents have told me they have girls as young as 3 who have asked to go on diets.

Tough Boys

Media culture frequently teaches boys that aggression is normal for them. Boys are supposed to be tough, ready to fight, and utterly self-reliant. Over and over in television programs, movies, video games, and media-linked toys marketed to young boys, violence provides an acceptable, even desirable, way to solve problems and feel powerful (Manganello & Taylor 2009).

Box 3.1

Letter to Parents About Birthday Parties for Girls

Dear Parents,

Several of you have asked about what kinds of birthday parties we would recommend you have for your daughters. We recommend parties that are age-appropriate for young girls, such as arts and crafts, games, or sports activities. We know that there are more and more "canned" and glitzy party possibilities out there for girls, often connected to what is currently popular in the media and popular culture. But we urge you to find an approach that provides girls with interesting, fun, age-appropriate activities. With these kinds of parties it is often easier and worthwhile to involve your daughter in the planning process.

We discourage parties that focus on aspects of a girl's appearance that are usually associated with teenagers and young adults. It is also worthwhile to listen to the lyrics of music played for dancing to ensure that the topics and words are appropriate for young children.

Finally, we ask parents to think carefully about the message that birthday themes and associated activities send to their daughter and her friends. We want all the girls to enjoy their special day and trust that there are many opportunities for family and close friends to celebrate in ways that don't affect school life. When school friends are included, we need to respect the diversity of the community, the core values inherent in education at our school, and the developmental levels of young children.

We are happy to answer any questions you may have about this message or your daughter's party planning.

Sincerely,

Instead of experiencing the *real* power that can come from having a meaningful impact in their environment and developing relationships with the people in it, boys instead often experience the *pseudo*-power that comes from the media violence they imitate. Believing they must be tough can cut off boys from the feelings of empathy for others that they need to develop in order to have mutually empowering relationships. The stereotypic messages of "Hurt, don't help" and "Be strong, don't ask anyone else for help" permeate this culture of masculinity. Although these types of messages have long been around, the pervasiveness of media messages today aimed at younger and younger boys has made them a bigger influence in early childhood.

The fighting that boys see on screens and in advertisements for toys and other media-linked products is worrisome. It helps explain the obsession with war play many teachers have described to me over the years since deregulation, when violence became a commonly used theme for marketing to boys. And research has shown that children who view a lot of entertainment violence are more likely to view violence as an effective way of settling conflicts, to become emotionally desensitized to violence in real life, and to develop the perception that the world is a violent and mean place (Huesmann, Dubow, & Yang 2013). In addition, children exposed to violent programming at a young age have a higher tendency for violent and aggressive behavior later in life than children who are not so exposed (American Academy of Pediatrics 2009).

The World Is a Dangerous Place

One of a child's most basic needs is to feel safe and secure. Although there are many children who live with actual violence, through today's media even children who do not live with violence are shown a world that is full of dangers, where bad things happen, where people do scary things, and in which you need to be ready to protect yourself. When children feel unsafe, they put more of their energy into trying to keep themselves free from harm. Feeling safe, however, allows children to put their energy into positive growth—into becoming autonomous, competent, and caring people who learn how to have a positive influence on their world. (For a detailed discussion of the importance of feeling safe for all aspects of healthy development and how to promote a sense of safety in children, see Levin 2003, 2010 in the Resources section.)

Age Compression

Age compression is a term used by media professionals and marketers to describe how children at ever-younger ages are doing what older children used to do. The media, toys, behavior, and clothing once seen as appropriate for teens are now firmly ensconced in the lives of many

---

Box 3.2

Age Compression in a Kindergarten–First Grade Classroom

Here are some comments one teacher overheard in her urban kindergarten–first grade classroom that exemplify age compression (McLaughlin 2009):

- "Yesterday after school Trina and Shayla got in a catfight over Brandon!"
- "My butt is hot!"
- "I got his phone number!"
- "She thinks she's cuter than me."

The teacher remarked, "These comments may or may not raise an eyebrow in any middle school classroom, but the year they became a common occurrence in my kindergarten and first grade classroom it threw me for a loop."

tweens and are rapidly encroaching on and influencing the lives of younger children. There is a blurring of boundaries between what children of different ages do and wear, which is often clearly demonstrated on screens in the similarities in clothing that girls and women wear. This clothing is marketed to both girls and women by the fashion industry.

When younger children try to imitate and behave like older children, they miss out on establishing the foundations needed to be ready for later experiences—at the appropriate age. They also cannot fully understand the more sophisticated behavior they are trying to engage in, which can lead to harmful experiences and lessons.

Undermining Adult Support: Premature Adolescent Rebellions

In the current media environment, children see more content that they need to process than ever before. Caring adults have a vital role to play in helping them do this, but media can weaken children's willingness to look to the important adults in their lives for nurturance and support. It often seems like media producers and marketers work to undermine caring adults' ability to perform this vital role.

What children often see in the media, especially in commercial children's television programming, is a world where "children know what's best." Many children in these programs seem to live in a world devoid of adults, where children function fully on their own. On the occasions when adults do appear, they are often portrayed as inept fools who are outsmarted by the children, or they create roadblocks to the things children want. It is possible that this is contributing to the phenomenon teachers and parents often tell me about of children who are beginning to rebel against adult authority—to start their adolescent rebellions—at younger and younger ages. The stars of these shows demonstrate how premature adolescent rebellions work, usually by ignoring adults and engaging in age compression behavior (Barbaro & Earp 2008; Linn 2005). In addition, media marketers do "nag factor" research on how to use advertising to get children to nag their parents for products that the parents often would not choose to buy otherwise (Briesch & Bridges 2006; Henry & Borzekowski 2011).

All of this can result in children's resisting the guidance of caring adults or rebelling against their parents (and teachers) long before they reach adolescence, when challenging the authority of adults is thought to be an important part of the self-identity process. Instead of seeking advice and support from their parents and teachers, children in the primary grades may turn to their peers and media idols for ideas about how to act. This can give media culture an even more powerful role in children's lives, which can make childhood more risky and both teaching and parenting more difficult.

Process Issues: Media Culture Affects *How* Children Learn

The problems media culture creates for some children do not come just from the content they see on screens. They also come from the *process* children are engaged in when they are connected to screens as well as the process they are *not* engaged in when they are connected. While children are glued to a screen, they are not actively engaged with their immediate real-world environment; they are not playing with real objects, exploring, or interacting with others around them; and they are not involved with their own agenda that they can control based on their own interests and needs.

Instead, screens often give children someone else's script that is designed to grab their attention, tell them what to do, and sell them things. This can become so engaging for children that on occasions when they are *not* directly involved with someone else's script, they often do not take the opportunity to become actively engaged in activities of their own making—such as playing with open-ended materials, looking at or reading books, and creating their own play scenarios. Rather, children gravitate to the media-linked and electronic toys that dominate the toy market and that are often highly realistic replicas of what they see on the screen. These toys tend to "remote control" children's play by supporting a more scripted play than children's self-directed creative play.

When repeatedly involved in this remote-controlled environment, children can easily become disconnected from the real-world, hands-on experiences that they most need for optimal development and learning. Their own ideas can seem boring compared to the excitement they see on the screen. This leads many children to prefer the fast-paced stimulation and immediate gratification of programs and interactive screens. And many parents have told me they often find that the more screen time their children have, the more they seem to want and even need.

Play Deficit Disorder

Play is vital to all aspects of children's development and learning. Children actively use play to master experience and skills and to try out new ideas and actions. In the process, they learn a lot about how to find interesting problems to work on and how to solve them in creative ways. This helps children feel the sense of mastery that comes from actively figuring things out on their own and learning new skills and ideas.

What children learn as they play is affected by *how* they play. When play arises from children's own imaginations, experiences, abilities, and needs, it is likely to more fully meet their social, emotional, and intellectual needs and to contribute to a solid foundation for later learning. It also teaches them *how to learn* as they work out their own problems and build their own understandings (Gray 2011; Levin & Carlsson-Paige 2006; Linn 2008; Miller & Almon 2009). When play arises from the influence of media, children's play reflects the scripts they have seen and not their own individual knowledge and experience or needs.

Many teachers (and parents) report that they have problems promoting children's creative play in their classrooms (or at home). They observe that when children have time for creative play, some often complain that they are bored and ask to watch television, play a video game, or play a tablet app or

While children are glued to a screen, they are not actively engaged with their immediate real-world environment.

Play Deficit Disorder: When given the opportunity to engage in open-ended play, children find it challenging to create their own play scenarios and often say they are bored. They also seem to have more conflicts with one another during play than children did in the past, and these conflicts often bring the play to a halt before it progresses very far. [*Note:* This term is meant to describe the impact of media on children, not as a label to be used for other purposes.]

For more information on the academic pushdown and what teachers can do about it, go to the Defending the Early Years website (www.deyproject.org).

game. Teachers have also told me that when children do play, they seem to have more conflicts with one another than children did in the past, conflicts that often bring the play to a halt before it progresses very far. I have termed these changes in children's play, *play deficit disorder*.

I believe that media culture is contributing to today's changes in children's play. As children spend more time with screens at home, many have less time to play with toys and outdoors. Similarly, in school there used to be opportunities for play with open-ended materials that allowed young children to develop problem-solving skills, learn about their environment, and begin to understand their world. The growing pressure on teachers to use technology to teach academic skills, meet performance standards, and administer tests at younger ages can crowd out opportunities for play.

When children do have time to play and materials to play with in school, their experiences with the highly realistic media-linked toys they use at home can make it difficult for some to create and play with the more open-ended materials available. Some children have trouble coming up with their own ideas for play.

Children who do not engage regularly in creative play are less likely to learn the important skills that creative play can teach (Levin 2011). They have a harder time coming up with their own interesting questions to answer or problems to figure out how to solve in play. They have fewer play strategies for solving the questions that arise as part of their play. When this happens, the foundation that is needed for all kinds of learning in school and beyond can be jeopardized. Furthermore, as these skills are undermined, we would expect to see children who have short attention spans, flit from activity to activity, and have difficulty engaging deeply during free play—indeed, these observations are very similar to those described in Box 3.3 on and by many other teachers.

Problem-Solving Deficit Disorder

Children who have difficulty engaging in creative play often have a hard time finding and solving meaningful problems on their own, an important ability that promotes the active construction of knowledge and skills. They seem to have what I have come to call *problem-solving deficit disorder*. These children have a hard time being active agents of their own learning or being involved with the world; for example, thinking of words that begin with the letter *b* or persuading another child to share a play material. They may often say they are bored and have trouble becoming deeply engaged in less structured, more open-ended activities. They may experience greater difficulty in

Box 3.3

A Teacher's Description of Play Deficit Disorder

Here is how one teacher of 4-year-olds described changes in her classroom over several years relative to children's play:

"It's harder and harder to have free play in my classroom. Some children can't cope with the lack of structure. They roam around the room dabbling with this or that, rarely getting involved in any activity for long. When they do, it often quickly dissolves into a conflict. I've stopped putting out some of the more traditional play materials, like playdough. Children don't do much with it; they just poke at it and then go on to something else. It's often easier to plan structured activities that I lead. Most of the kids do what I tell them to do; I worry about what they aren't learning when I do that."

playing cooperatively with others or resolving conflicts without aggression.

Children who exhibit these characteristics often do better when they are told what to do—that is, when they have structured activities at school or DVDs to watch and video games to play at home. They often ask for new things but quickly become bored once they get them. Many parents tell me that screen activities seem to be their children's favorite thing to do, yet many are not aware of how screens became so central to their children's lives.

A reliance on screens and media-related scripts can undermine optimal academic learning as well as inhibit children from learning how to solve conflicts and social problems with others. In the long run, I believe that it can encourage children to conform to others' ideas and accept directions without question. It may also mean that children miss out on the joy that can come from figuring out how to solve an interesting problem on their own and the sense of personal power that this can bring. Research is very much needed to explore the relationship between the decline of quality play, children's ability to problem solve, and the rapid rise of mandates for more teaching of basic academic skills at younger ages (Strauss 2012).

Compassion Deficit Disorder

Children learn how to interact positively with others from their personal experiences in the social realm—for instance, how they are treated, how they see people treating one another, and through adult modeling and support. They very gradually learn what to say and do to peacefully work out problems with others and to have respectful give-and-take relationships. It is vital that children have experiences that help them learn these skills when they are young because research has found that exposure to violent media content before age 9, without intervention, is predictive of aggressive behavior in adulthood (Eron, Gentry, & Schlegel 1994; Huesmann et al. 2003).

Screen time takes time away from learning how to interact with others in the real world. Such experiences provide immediate, direct feedback on the impact of one's actions. When children have far fewer opportunities to learn positive social behavior from direct experience, they can be deprived of developing increasingly reciprocal and empathic social skills.

Such a decline in social skills can be heightened when combined with the media's messages of violence, aggression, and mean-spirited behavior as well as sex, sexualization, and a focus on appearance. The media culture frequently supports a stereotypic view that, for girls, the basis of relationships is how they look and the things they have, rather than their connection to others. And media culture teaches boys to judge themselves and one another based on how strong, independent, and ready to fight they are, not by their positive connections with others. In a sense, both girls and boys are made into *objects*. Objectification of self and others makes it much easier to act in mean and uncaring ways in relationships.

This objectification can create a disturbing gap in children's social development that I have termed *compassion deficit disorder* (Levin 2008). It describes

Problem-Solving Deficit Disorder: When children find it challenging to engage deeply in unstructured activities, have a difficult time playing with others cooperatively, and prefer structured activities and being told what to do. [*Note*: This term is meant to describe the impact of media on children, not as a label to be used for other purposes.]

Compassion Deficit Disorder: When children are less able to take the point of view of others, to understand or be concerned about how their actions affect others, or to experience empathy. [*Note*: This term is meant to describe the impact of media on children, not as a label to be used for other purposes.]

the behavior of children who may be less able to take the point of view of others, to understand or be concerned about how their actions affect others, or to experience empathy. What often results from this gap are accounts like the ones in Box 3.4, from a teacher of 6-year-olds and a teacher of third grade students.

Many teachers tell me they spend a great deal of time trying to maintain a sense of safety in their classrooms and admit to resorting to more time-outs and harsher discipline techniques than in the past. They also say they are seeing younger children exhibit the kind of bullying and teasing that used to be characteristic of older children (another example of age compression). An apparent increase in antisocial behavior has led some schools to abolish recess because children are hurting each other on the playground (Bornstein 2011).

The amount of television viewing at age 4 has been found to be associated with subsequent bullying (Zimmerman et al. 2005). This finding led the authors to conclude that exposure to television in the home environment in the early years has a significant impact on bullying in grade school. As young children's involvement with screens has continued to increase since that study, new research is needed that explores the effects of screens on young children's bullying behavior as well as the possible reasons for this correlation. Could it be that, as children have less firsthand experience with others because of the time they spend with screens, it is more difficult for them to develop the social skills they need to learn about the effects of their actions on others?

There are certainly other societal as well as personal factors that are affecting children's development of compassion and other interpersonal skills. However, regardless of the causes, we need to intentionally help children develop positive social skills and show compassion, just as we help them learn physical or cognitive skills. Part Two of this book outlines strategies for countering the impact of media culture on children, including developing relationships in the classroom and teaching children media literacy skills.

Culture Clash

As I have come to identify and understand the complex ways that the new technological age is affecting children's development and learning, it often seems as if children are growing up in two separate, disconnected cultures. One is filled with the attitudes, values, and behaviors many teachers and parents try to instill—what we believe children need to learn in order to grow up to be caring, fulfilled, contributing members of society. I call this the family–school–societal culture. The other is filled with messages children encounter through media—much of which teaches the types of worrisome content and process lessons outlined previously in this chapter. I have found it helpful to visualize these two cultures as two disconnected boxes in children's heads (see Figure 3.1). For many children, the two boxes and the information in them are deeply at odds with each other.

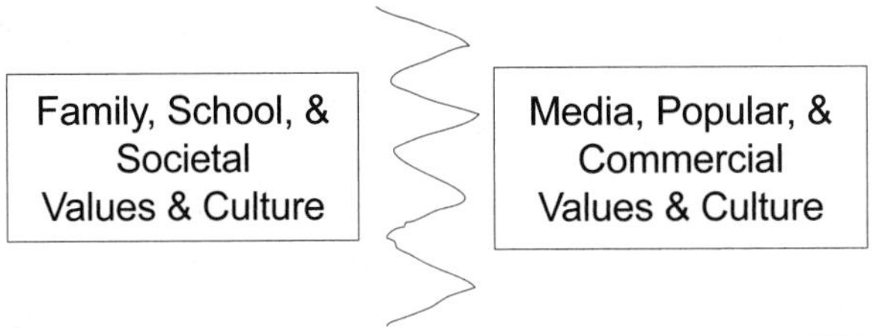

Figure 3.1 **Clash of Cultures**

| Family, School, & Societal Values & Culture | Media, Popular, & Commercial Values & Culture |

As negative media influences increase, the media culture box grows larger, and the family–school–societal culture box can get crowded out. On their own, because of how young children think, it can be difficult for children to connect the content in the two boxes or make it into an integrated whole. They go back and forth between the two boxes, depending on the demands of the current situation. Not surprisingly, conflicts can easily occur when adults who care for and educate children are operating in the family–school–societal culture box and children are operating in the media culture box.

Beyond Remote-Controlled Childhood

Because the pervasiveness of today's media-saturated environment creates cause for concern, we need to ask whether there is any positive role that media can play in young children's lives. I strongly believe that the answer depends on 1) the extent to which we can find media that does *not* contribute to the kinds of content and process issues described in this chapter and 2) what adults do to help children think about, use, and regulate the media in their lives. In other words, we need to find media that predominately connects to the family–school–societal culture box—*not* the media culture box.

Box 3.5 on page 40 illustrates appropriate and inappropriate media and how each relates to children's key developmental needs. You can also use this information to identify the types of media messages to which the children in your program may be exposed.

Ideally, to help children get beyond remote-controlled childhood, we need to look for media and screen activities that help children engage positively with the issues most basic to healthy social, emotional, and intellectual development (i.e., the issues in the family–school–societal culture box), and that avoid those aspects of media that undermine development (i.e., the harmful issues in the media culture box).

When we cannot find the ideal, the question becomes this: Are there ways adults can help children transform the media lessons they learn that undermine their development and learning into lessons that support children's development and learning? If the answer is yes, then the experience can be appropriate. If the answer is no, then to the extent

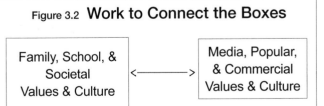

Figure 3.2 **Work to Connect the Boxes**

| Family, School, & Societal Values & Culture | <———> | Media, Popular, & Commercial Values & Culture |

possible, we should try to keep children from the exposure. And if children are exposed anyway, as explained in Part Two of this book, there is much we can do to counteract the potential negative impact.

The remaining chapters of this book will help you become more effective at helping young children get beyond remote-controlled experiences. This will involve helping children and their families make the family–school–societal culture box as large as possible while reducing the size of the media culture box. It also requires helping children connect the content of the two boxes so they don't feel as if they are living in two separate worlds, as illustrated in Figure 3.2 on page 39.

Box 3.5

Developmental Framework for Assessing the Media in Young Children's Lives

Explore some of the media and screen activities that are most popular with the children in your program, and try to figure out how what you see fits into the following developmental framework.

Key Developmental Need	Inappropriate Media Message	Appropriate Media Message
To establish a sense of **trust and safety**	The world is dangerous; enemies are everywhere; weapons and fighting are needed to feel safe.	Many people can be trusted and will help you; safety and predictability can be achieved.
To develop a sense of **autonomy with connectedness**	Autonomy is equated with physical and verbal fighting. Connectedness is equated with helplessness, weakness, and altruism.	You can do positive things to meet your needs. Provides concrete examples of how others can help you and you can help them.
To establish **gender identity**	Portrays exaggerated, rigid gender divisions and behaviors. Boys are strong, ready to fight, and save the world. Girls are pretty, sexy, and need the right bodies and clothes to be successful.	Portrays complex characters with wide-ranging behaviors, interests, and skills. There are commonalties between boys and girls and overlap in what both can do.
To learn to **appreciate similarities and differences** among people	Portrays racial, ethnic, and class stereotypes and dehumanized enemies. Diversity is undesirable, even dangerous. Violence against those who are different is okay.	There is exposure to diverse peoples with varied talents, skills, and needs who treat each other with respect, work out problems peacefully, and enrich each other's lives.
To build the foundations of **morality and social responsibility**	Portrays one-dimensional characters who are either all good or all bad. Violence is the solution to problems. Winning and losing are the only possible outcomes. Bad people deserve to be hurt.	Portrays complex characters who act responsibly and morally toward others, show kindness and respect, work out moral problems, and take other people's points of view and needs into account.

Box 3.5 cont'd

Key Developmental Need	Inappropriate Media Message	Appropriate Media Message
To **play in child-constructed, age-appropriate, creative** ways	Program content is removed from children's experience or level of understanding. Toys linked to programs promoting imitation, not creative play. Playtime reduced by screen time.	There is meaningful content for children to bring into their play that resonates deeply with developmental level and needs. Shows are not linked to realistic toys so children can create their own unique play with open-ended toys.
To engage in meaningful **problem finding and problem solving**	Shows an onslaught of quick-paced actions and solutions, with little opportunity to see concrete cause-and-effect connections to problems in the real world.	Shows examples of meaningful problem finding and problem solving of age-appropriate issues. Includes ideas for engaging interesting problems to work on in the real world.
To get deep **satisfaction from personal mastery** and accomplishment	Conveys that buying and getting the right things brings happiness, popularity, and success. One's energy needs to go into discovering the right things and trying to obtain them.	Conveys that there are many challenges to master in the world, and it feels really good to use what you already know to accomplish something new.
To be involved with **age-appropriate content and activities**	Strive to be a teenager and do teenager activities. Try to be as grown up as possible, not a child.	There are many ways to have fun and get satisfaction from being a child and doing concrete, hands-on activities.
To see **caring adults as a valuable source of help** and guidance	Children know what's best. You don't need adults to help you. Adults often get in the way of doing what will make you happy.	Adults and children are shown in caring and connected relationships. Adults are there to help you meet your needs and assist you when you have problems.
To learn to appreciate and enjoy the slow and **steady pace of real-life activities**	Action is fast paced. Instant gratification and solutions, without connection to real-world efforts.	Situations connected to real life and closer to the actual pace of life. Gradual results from meaningful efforts.

Adapted from D. Levin and N. Carlsson-Paige, "Developmentally Appropriate Television: Putting Children First," *Young Children* 49 (July 1994): 38–44.

It's Worth the Effort

For those of you who feel that I am adding yet another demand to your already too demanding job, you are correct! In the long run, however, you will find that understanding and working proactively to help children growing up in the media age will make your teaching less stressful, more effective, and yes, more satisfying!

Setting the Stage: Learn More About the Media in Young Children's Lives

4

Finding ways to make a positive, lasting impact on the media-saturated environment in which children live and develop is a challenging endeavor. The more you know about media and how it influences the children with whom you work, the more proactive you can be at enhancing its positive aspects and reducing the negative aspects.

Promoting children's healthy development, learning, and behavior is an ongoing process, especially with the impact of today's ever-changing media and popular culture. The picture is further complicated by the unique ways each child makes sense of the media around her and by the attitudes that families have about media culture. A flexible, multifaceted approach that adapts to the changes in children's lives will help you handle media and media-related issues effectively, beginning with knowing about the specific media in each child's life. This knowledge will help you do the following:

- Identify what and how media and media-related issues are influencing children's thoughts and behavior

- Have meaningful discussions about media issues with the children and their families

- Develop positive approaches for working with children based on their specific issues and needs

Strategies for Learning About the Media in Young Children's Lives

Here are some key steps you and your colleagues can take to develop a foundation for helping children make sense of what they see, hear, and do with the electronic media in their lives.

Show Your Interest in Children's Media Usage

Develop a supportive environment in which you connect and stay connected with children around media and technology in their lives. Convey to the children your desire to learn more about their interests in and involvement with media. This means helping children feel that they will not be judged or criticized for raising media-related topics and, therefore, that they are free to say what they think and know from their screen experiences. This is how you will learn what you need to know to develop strategies for working with children around both the positive and negative impacts of media and media culture. If issues do come up that concern you, take note of them so you can devise ways to handle them thoughtfully and effectively. The rest of this book is filled with strategies to help you do this. One simple way to begin connecting with children about media is to say something like, "Tell me what you know about that character [or game or program]," when a child mentions something he saw on a screen.

Learn more about the media and technology that children seem to care about most. During individual conversations and group meetings, ask the children in your class about the media that may have come up in their classroom conversations—the television programs, video and computer games, apps, and other media that are currently important to them. Be alert for media-related topics to arise during children's play. Engage children in discussions about these, but try to do so in a way that does not interfere with the play. Once you begin connecting more with children about the media they mention, and they know this is something that interests rather than upsets you, it will begin to feel more natural to them to connect with you when you initiate media-related conversations. Here are further steps you can take to learn what the children are exposed to through media culture:

◆ Keep notes on the key media- and technology-related issues that come up in children's conversations and play.

◆ Once you know what media is most on children's minds, learn more about it. If it's a television program, movie, or game, watch it or play it by yourself or, even better, with other teachers and/or parents so that you can discuss it together. Analyze how what you learn relates to how you have seen the content affecting children, and then develop strategies for working with and talking to children about it. (Refer to Box 3.5, Developmental Framework for Assessing the Media in Young Children's Lives, in Chapter 3 to help you determine what kind of messages children may be getting from their exposure to media.)

◆ Make sure you know about the other kinds of media that the children talk about, such as video and computer games, smartphone or tablet apps, websites, and online virtual communities for young children. Again, investigate them yourself.

◆ Learn about the various rating systems for television programs, movies, and video games. These give you a starting point for knowing when children may be consuming content that has been rated for older children or adults. It can also help you identify issues you might want to address together with the children's families. Be aware that these rating systems are limited; as noted in a report on three studies of parents' discontent with media rating systems (Gordon 2011), they do not provide specific information on content.

◆ Each form of media has a different rating system, so you will often find a movie with a rating for one age and the connected TV show with a rating for younger or older children. Keep these points in mind:

- Individuals who assign the ratings do not necessarily have special knowledge of child development or other appropriate training. For example, the movie industry uses members of the public to assign ratings to films.

- There are no formal guidelines for assigning age recommendations for toys. This is up to individual manufacturers. This means that a movie rated PG-13 or even R can have a toy linked to it that is recommended for young children.

- As of this writing, only Common Sense Media has a rating system for apps, the use of which is growing rapidly among young children. This organization also provides information about other types of rating systems.

Ask families to complete the Media Profile Questionnaire so you can learn more about the role media and media culture play in the children's lives. This survey, which appears at the end of this chapter along with a letter to parents, can help you identify families' use of technology at home, how they feel about the use of technology in their families, and their attitudes about how media culture is affecting their children. You can use families' responses to set goals and develop strategies for promoting reflection and discussion (and if appropriate, change) among family members and between family members and you. In many cases, the very process of completing the questionnaire will start this reflection and discussion process.

Box 4.1
Where to Find Media Rating Systems
- Television program rating system: www.tvguidelines.org
- Movie rating system: www.mpaa.org/ratings/what-each-rating-means
- Ratings of movies, games, apps, websites, television programs, books, and music: Common Sense Media at www.commonsensemedia.org

Use what you learn from the completed questionnaires to tailor your response to the special characteristics, experiences, and attitudes of your children and families. For example, suppose some of the parents express concern that their children spend too much time with screens and indicate that their children have trouble developing nonscreen interests at home. In response, you might focus on helping children develop play interests at school that they can connect to play at home—for example, using playdough at school and then sending home the recipe for how to make it. Many of the activities in the following chapters can be shaped to address issues raised in the completed questionnaires.

Stay Informed About Screen Media and Media Culture

Learn more about the specific screen devices children use.

◆ Visit stores that sell technology. Look for demonstration models of items that children have mentioned. Try using different games and apps to learn more about what's involved when children use them. As you explore, think about what the children have said about them. Try to put yourself in their shoes. What is the lure of this particular device or content? What might it mean to them? What skills are they using and not using when they interact with it? What might they be learning from the experience?

◆ Search the Internet to find more information about the features, uses, drawbacks, and benefits of specific devices.

Learn about the popular media-linked toys children have and use the most, and what they do with them. Even if your program does not have media-linked toys among its curriculum materials and does not allow children to bring toys from home, the use of these toys will affect what and how children play at school. Knowing about the role of these toys in children's out-of-school play, then, can help you better understand how media is entering their lives and what messages they may be learning from it. This knowledge will also help you respond to media-related issues in the classroom. (The topic of media, toys, and play is discussed more fully in Chapter 7.) Here are some suggestions for learning about the toys that are popular with the children in your class.

◆ Visit a mass market toy store or the toy department of a retail chain store to survey toys currently marketed to children in the age range you teach.

  • Notice the toys featured in special displays.

  • Read the descriptions on the backs of toy boxes.

  • Try to figure out which toys are marketed to boys and which are marketed to girls. How could you tell? What do the toys tell children about how they should play with the toys? What might children learn from the toy—and the media to which the toy is connected?

  • Observe interactions among children and adults in the store to see what toys they choose, how they choose them, and what they talk about as they decide.

◆ Search the Web for the toys that are most popular with the children in your class to learn more about their online marketing.

Learn more about the nature and role of media-linked products beyond toys (such as clothing, food products, lunch boxes, and shoes) in children's lives.

◆ Search online to see what other products are tied to the most popular media targeted to children. It can be quite overwhelming to see the amount and variety, but this information is helpful in understanding the current forces that are affecting children.

◆ To keep current with media-linked products, once a week ask yourself these questions:

- What products with media logos did children bring to school this week?

- What do children say when they talk about these products?

- How and when do these products come up in children's play?

- Do issues ever arise between children about who has what item or who wants what item?

The story described at the beginning of Chapter 1, about the young girl who was not allowed to eat lunch at the princess table because she hadn't brought her princess lunch box to school, offers a dramatic example of the kind of information you might collect—and the type of situations you need to address.

Use What You Know to Act

Use what you discover about the nature and impact of children's media and the use of technology from this book and your own research to make *informed* and *intentional* decisions about *if* and *how* you will use technology in your classroom. As technology becomes more and more prevalent in settings for young children, think carefully about which screen devices you will use in your own classroom, if you have that choice. Be clear as to *why* you are using the media you choose, the *guidelines* you will implement to enable children to be engaged and creative learners when they use screen devices, and *how* the technology will contribute to children's learning in ways that concrete classroom materials cannot.

Deciding not to use technology is also a viable option in many settings. Many children, especially those who have a lot of screen time at home, may benefit from not having screens to distract them from hands-on activities when they are in group settings (Campaign for a Commercial-Free Childhood, Alliance for Childhood, & Teachers Resisting Unhealthy Children's Entertainment 2012). Whether or not you decide to use screens, it is important to still work intentionally to learn about and address, wherever possible, the effects of media on young children. (For more help deciding whether or not to use technology and, if so, how to use it, see *Facing the Screen Dilemma*, listed in the Resources section.)

Use the ideas in this book to help families, programs, and the wider community work together to deal positively with media-related issues that affect children. It can be very difficult as a teacher or parent to work on these issues in isolation. Sharing ideas, successes, and failures with others will encourage you in your efforts and help you develop effective strategies tailored to your program's unique circumstances. Positively influencing children's developing ideas and behaviors is also much easier when the adults in their lives work together.

Learn more about the devices and media-linked products in children's lives.

In my own efforts to get others involved, I have found almost nothing but appreciation and relief when other adults discover structured and manageable ways to make informed decisions about the media in children's lives and to work effectively with children on these issues. (Part Three of this book provides many resources and strategies to help you in this effort.) Here are a few ways to begin collaborating with colleagues and families:

◆ Organize meetings to work with families and/or other teachers on the ideas in this book that seem most relevant to your situation.

◆ If your setting has a regular newsletter for families, contribute articles about media issues that inform and engage families.

◆ To better understand the appeal and effects of media and technology, examine the role they play in your own life. Use the following questions to explore your own experiences, and those of your family, with media.

• What media and technology do I use, and when do I use it?

• How do media and technology contribute to and detract from my work and my life outside of work?

• What role do media and technology play in my relationships with family members and friends? How do they affect the way we spend time together and what we like to talk about?

• Are there things about the media in my life I would like to change? If so, why? What and how can I begin to make these changes?

• How can my own experiences with media and my feelings about its role in my life help me better understand the media experiences of the children in my class and their families?

Box 4.2

Media Profile Letter

Dear Parents,

I often hear children talk about watching television programs or movies, playing video games, and engaging in other screen activities at home. Sometimes what children see, hear, and do while they are involved with screens affects their learning and how they act with each other—sometimes in ways that are positive, and other times in ways that may not be positive. I want to develop strategies in the classroom that promote the positive aspects of children's use of screen devices and limit any negative aspects. To accomplish this task, it would help me to know more about how your child uses screen devices at home. Please answer the questions on the survey as best you can, and return it to me. Please be assured that there are no right or wrong, good or bad answers.

I appreciate your help. I will share more about what we do in the classroom around this issue in the future.

Sincerely,

Box 4.3

Use of Screen Media at Home   Child's Name _____

1. What kind of media does your child use at home? Some examples are TV, DVDs, computer and video games, the Internet, and apps.

2. What kind of technology does your child use at home? Examples are smartphones, tablets, music players such as iPods, and ebook readers.

3. About how many hours a day does your child uses screens and screen-related activities?

4. What times of day or days of the week does your child most often use screen devices?

5. What are the main places your child uses screen devices? Some examples are the family room, bedroom, kitchen, the car, or at a friend's or relative's house.

6. What kinds of TV programs and other screen activities are your child's favorites?

7. What does your child like to do when he or she is not watching TV or using other screen devices?

8. Does your family spend time together watching TV or DVDs, using computers, or doing other screen activities? If so, please describe.

9. What are the activities that your family likes to do together that do not involve a TV, computer, or other screen? If so, please describe.

10. When other children come to your home to play with your child, do the children use technology when they play? If they do, what technology do they use? Examples include televisions, video game consoles, tablets, and smartphones.

11. Do you have any rules about what programs, games, or other screen activities your child can watch or use, such as when, or for how long? If so, what are the rules? How well do you feel they are working?

12. What are your children's favorite toys? Are any of them electronic? Are any of them linked to TV shows, movies, or other media?

13. What benefits do you see as from your child's use of TV, computer and video games, and other screen activities? What, if any, negative effects do you see? Is there anything you would like to learn more about or change? If so, please describe.

14. If you have more than one child, what are their ages? If yes, do the children's different ages create any challenges for your family's media use? Please explain.

15. Are there any issues related to media that you hope we will address in the classroom or that you want to learn more about? If so, please explain.

16. Is there anything else you would like to say about media in your child's and your family's life?

Helping Children Get Beyond Remote-Controlled Childhood in Classroom Settings

PART TWO

Problem Solving With Children: How One Teacher Helped the Princesses and Princes Live Happily Ever After

Problem Solving With Children: How One Teacher Helped the Princesses and Princes Live Happily Ever After

What children see and hear and experience through media often finds its way into their play in the classroom. Some play inspired by children's media experiences may be limited in imagination and creativity, and at times it may lead to conflicts between children. This chapter presents an example of the impact of media on children in a preschool classroom and illustrates how the teacher addressed it. This example involved princess play, but the principles discussed can be applied to other media-influenced situations as well. It illustrates the kinds of goals and action strategies that are discussed in greater depth in the chapters that follow.

Trouble in the Kingdom

For the last few years, princesses have been a common play theme and topic of conversation among the 4-year-old girls in Hilda's classroom. She has never been fond of this emphasis on princesses, but since the children usually quickly move on to other play themes that are more imaginative and complex, Hilda has not considered it to be an issue.

But this year, after the December holiday break, several girls arrived with new enthusiasm for princesses. There was much discussion over who had seen which princess movies over the break and who had gotten which princess toys and other products. For the first time, two girls started bringing their lunch to school in princess lunch boxes.

Soon the dramatic play area was taken over by the new princess enthusiasts. Other girls, who hadn't paid much attention in the past to classroom princess activities, began to join in. Many conflicts arose over who could wear which dress-up clothes and who could pretend to be which princess. But once the girls were dressed up, it didn't seem like they had a lot they wanted to do; Hilda didn't see much meaningful dramatic play develop. In addition, the boys who had previously played in the dramatic play area with the girls now avoided it. Sitting together at snack time, girls would often talk about princess movies they wanted to see and which toys or other products they had heard about and wanted to get next. It began to feel to Hilda as if princesses were taking over more and more of classroom life.

The princess play affected the children's outdoor time too. The girls started chasing boys, catching them, and designating them as their princes. They would hang on to the boys and drag them around the playground. Although a few boys didn't seem to mind, and even liked the attention, several boys had fights with the girls because they wanted to be left alone.

Then the princesses began having regular conversations about which boys were the "best" princes, and Hilda started hearing mean comments about the boys the girls didn't want as their princes. The rejected princes were generally the younger, more sensitive boys. The preferred boys started acting like they had experienced some sort of victory.

In turn, the princes began talking about who were "good" and who were "bad" princesses—generally, the thin, femininely dressed girls who often dominated the play were considered the good princesses. Snack time became a time for children to discuss who they wanted to be and *not* to be their prince or princess when they went outside. Some of the children who were not chosen did not seem to care, although some looked upset.

Hilda was increasingly concerned about what was going on and began thinking about how to get more involved. In the past, she had addressed each princess or prince problem as it arose. If a girl pressured a boy to be "her prince" and the boy objected, then Hilda would talk with the girl about needing to respect the boy's wishes and leave him alone.

Hilda pondered her options. Should she ban princesses and princes from school entirely? That wasn't how she had dealt with problems like this in the past, and she recognized that banning the play wouldn't address the issues that were making princesses so central to so many of the girls' lives at home and at school, or with the lessons the girls were learning through their princess play. She also suspected that banning the play might lead to the children's finding more creative ways to go about it without Hilda knowing. Banning princesses and princes altogether didn't seem to be a valid option.

With some trepidation, Hilda decided that she needed to develop a more comprehensive approach for dealing with the princess play. The approach had to feel safe for everyone, be connected to the children's interests, and counteract what many of the children—especially the girls—seemed to be learning from the infusion of princesses into their world.

Here are the central questions that helped frame Hilda's efforts:

◆ What is it about girls pretending to be princesses in the classroom that makes me so uncomfortable?

◆ What is it about the princesses that appeals so deeply to the girls?

◆ Which girls are most drawn to the play, and what particular issues might be going on with them?

◆ Which issues surrounding the princess play seem most important to address in the classroom?

◆ How do families feel about the role of princesses in their daughters' lives, and how could I work together with them to connect what is happening at school with what might be happening at home?

◆ How can I connect with the children about the princess issue in ways that are meaningful to them and their needs and that will help to rebuild a positive classroom climate?

◆ How can I work with the children to expand the narrow stereotypical gender roles princesses are creating for both the girls and boys?

Hilda decided to start by having a nonjudgmental conversation with all the children about what was happening with princesses and princes in the classroom. This would allow Hilda to learn what the children were thinking, convey to them that she was interested in hearing their ideas, and assure them that it was safe to talk about their ideas. Boxes 5.1 on page 56 and 5.2 on page 58 show what Hilda and the class discussed during the course of two class meetings. The accompanying commentary points out the goals and strategies Hilda had in mind as she worked with the children. It also identifies what she learned from the children's comments and how she used them to help shape her responses.

Why This Approach?

This was a very difficult conversation for the teacher to lead, but Hilda found it interesting and productive. Her efforts powerfully illustrate what it means to help children get beyond remote-controlled childhood in today's world. There is no magic wand, princesses or not! She connects deeply with the children, begins where they are, and helps them bridge the chasm between the two conflicting cultures in which they are growing up—the media culture and the family–school–societal culture (see Chapter 3).

Both class discussions build on the children's experiences, thoughts, and feelings around a media culture issue about which many of them have very strong feelings. Because Hilda is careful to accept what they say without judgment and to encourage everyone to express their opinions, the children feel safe voicing their ideas. She views the process the children go through not just as an essential part of constructing a solution but as important in itself. It is an ongoing process in which potential solutions will be tried, evaluated, and modified. In sum, Hilda is promoting the attitudes, values, and skills that help counteract the negative impacts of media culture on children.

A nonjudgmental conversation with all the children would allow Hilda to learn what the children were thinking, convey her interest, and assure them that it was safe to talk about their ideas.

Box 5.1

Class Meeting 1: Introducing the Princess Problem

Dialogue	Commentary
Hilda: I've noticed something that seems to be causing problems in our classroom. A lot of you like to play princess in dress-up and outside. But a lot of the times when you do, there are classmates who get upset because they can't be the princess they want, or someone tells them they can't play. We need to figure out what to do so it feels better for everyone.	Hilda frames the discussion as a problem they all need to solve together. She chooses two salient issues to focus on: 1) the problem of children who are not getting to be the princesses they want and 2) the fact that some children are being told they can't play.
Gillian: I'm Snow White. I like her.	Gillian's comment is egocentric and focused on what she likes, not on others in the group. This egocentrism reflects her developmental stage—what Piaget termed the preoperational stage. During this stage, from 2 to 7 years old, children's thoughts and communication are usually centered on themselves and reflect only their own point of view.
Rhonda: I am always Cinderella. That's my favorite.	Rhonda, too, shows egocentrism and is focused on her own experience.
Hilda: So it sounds like you don't have a problem, Gillian and Rhonda. Anyone else? [Several hands go up.]	She accepts what Gillian and Rhonda say and doesn't judge them. She wants the children to say what they think, not to feel like there's a "right" answer.
Haley: I want to be Cinderella and she won't let me. She says there can't be two Cinderellas! [She points to Rhonda, who gives her a mean look. Haley looks like she's holding back tears.]	Distressed feelings and blame quickly emerge. Haley focuses on what happened to her. She thinks there can be two Cinderellas. Rhonda is a more literal thinker than Haley and thinks there can be only one Cinderella.
Hilda: So you want a chance to be Cinderella, the princess you like a lot. You wish there could be two? [Haley nods in agreement.] I know Rhonda really does like to be Cinderella, but you think it's okay to have two instead of taking turns? [Haley nods.]	Hilda reflects back what Haley said and then tries to help the children expand their understanding by bringing in both girls' points of view.
Rhonda: Well, there is only one! And she [Haley] doesn't look right anyway. I have blonde hair.	Rhonda's response is concrete, literal, and egocentric. She, and many of the other children, will need some help to consider possible solutions that work for everyone.
Hilda: So you think there can be only one Cinderella, and she needs to have the right color hair? What do others think?	Hilda doesn't pass judgment on Rhonda's comments. She reflects them back and invites other children to share their points of view.
Julia: That's mean. You can't make the color of your hair.	Julia shows a logical and less literal way of thinking. It focuses on one thing at a time. Just the kind of answer Hilda had hoped for!
Henry: Yeah, they are mean. We can't play. They won't let us! [A few boys nod in agreement.]	The word "mean" in Julia's comment triggers other children's experiences about being treated meanly. Now the larger issue Hilda wants to address has come up.

Dialogue	Commentary	Box 5.1 cont'd
Hilda: It sounds like you've had a problem too, Henry. Can you tell us more?	Hilda accepts Henry's distress without judgment, frames it as a problem, and asks him to expand so there is more for everyone to hear and talk about.	
Henry: In the playhouse, they say there can only be the princes *they* choose. It's not fair! Everyone should be able to be one. [More hands go up to speak.]	In his egocentric way (e.g., his use of the general term "they" instead of referring to specific children), Henry puts more pieces of the situation together. He raises the issue of justice.	
Hilda: You don't like it when they tell you what prince you have to be? Raise your hand if you haven't been able to be the prince or princess you want to be. [At least half of the hands go up.] Now, raise your hand if you can't play when you want to play. [Again, a lot of hands go up.]	Hilda summarizes Henry's key point and brings others into the discussion by giving them a concrete way to participate as a group—raising hands.	
Hilda: It sounds like a lot of you agree that we really do have a *problem*—you aren't happy with what's happening with the princes and princesses at school.	Hilda returns to her original framing of the situation and summarizes the problem so the children have something concrete to address.	
Sandy: I don't want to be a prince. It's stupid. It's for girls. [Several boys nod in agreement. Others disagree.]	Sandy shows that even within the rejected group, there are differing opinions. And he seems to feel safe saying what he really thinks.	
Hilda: So that's another part of the problem. We disagree about who should play and who shouldn't. You know how we've talked before about ways girls and boys can play together—like on the slide or in the block area. [Several nods.]	Hilda continues to help children expand their understanding of the problem: who is and isn't allowed to play. But she also connects the problem to gender issues and what they have done together in the past to address these issues.	
Jules: Yeah, but not princesses. Boys shouldn't have to do that!	Jules uses dichotomous, concrete thinking. He keeps what he previously learned about gender in a separate compartment from the prince and princess gender roles being discussed now.	
Hilda: Yes, Jules, we've talked before about how children shouldn't have to play what they don't want to play. But what I'm hearing now is that a lot of you are having problems with the princes and princesses at school. Sometimes children are mean to each other. It doesn't feel good. [There are nods of agreement, but a few children look worried.]	Hilda acknowledges what Jules says without correcting or passing judgment. Then, in an effort to stay focused on the key problem she hopes to work on, she brings the topic back to the current situation and how it feels to children. But she makes a note to herself to work more on the gender issues later.	
Hilda: We need to think about what we can do to try to make things feel better. You know—how we've come up with ideas before about how to change something or do something new when we had a problem. [She pauses, looking around at the children.] We've been sitting for a long time. I'm glad we've figured out more about our problem now. Let's have snack and think about what we can do. After snack and before we go outside, we can talk about your ideas and decide what to try. [As the children jump up to go to snack, some conversations are starting.]	Rather than trying to cover all the issues in one conversation, Hilda brings things back to addressing the problem in a way that helps everyone feel okay. Hilda sees the children are beginning to get restless, so she summarizes where they are with the problem and suggests a break. But she helps them plan ahead in a concrete way for what will come next—discussing and agreeing on a solution.	

Box 5.2

Class Meeting 2: Solving the Princess Problem

Dialogue	Commentary
Hilda: I heard some of you talking during snack about what we can do about princesses. Can you tell us all some of your ideas? I'll write them here on the whiteboard to help us remember them and decide which ones to try.	Hilda starts by using the children's ideas to brainstorm possible solutions. Although most of the children can't read all of what she writes, she writes down their ideas so they will know they'll be used later (a meaningful literacy activity).
Heather: No princesses. I don't like them! [A few loud groans are heard from the most devoted princesses.]	Heather's egocentric solution takes into account only her own wishes, which is okay when brainstorming. Despite the groans, Hilda continues the brainstorming.
Gillian: You can't say that . . . it's *not* fair.	Gillian brings in the idea of fairness to object to Heather's idea.
Hilda: Heather, it sounds like you wish there weren't princesses. But, Gillian sure doesn't like that idea. Let's see if we come up with things to try that will help *everyone* feel okay.	Hilda points out two different points of view without passing judgment on either. Then she reassures both children by repeating the goal of the meeting—trying to come up with a solution that works for everyone.
Gillian: We need to have princesses. We could all play princesses and princes outside.	Gillian is still pro-princess but suggests a solution that takes into account Hilda's stated goal and previous discussion.
Natasha: There aren't that many princesses! And how can we choose our princes if there are so many?	Natasha focuses on a literal fact—the number of princesses she knows (i.e., popular media princesses). But she makes a logical-causal connection imagining what would happen if the class tried to put Gillian's solution into practice.
Haley: That's why we can have two! Two of each princess. Then there's enough.	Haley is sticking with her idea from the first meeting—two Cinderellas. Now, she's expanded the idea to help solve the problem of having enough princess roles for everyone.
Hilda: So one solution would be to let everyone be a princess who wants to be one. And we could have two—a pair—of each princess so there are enough princesses. What do the two princesses do? Do they do things together or can they do different things?	Hilda combines several of the children's suggestions to help them see how they are linked and where their solutions might be taking them. She also channels the discussion to the specifics of how pairs of the same princesses will play.
Gillian: I think there can only be one of each, like in the movie.	As at the first meeting, Gillian has a hard time getting beyond the literal connection between the movie and the children's play.
Henry: You could have one day for each.	Henry jumps in with the start of a logical solution to Gillian's problem. He's definitely engaged in the discussion.

Dialogue	Commentary	Box 5.2 cont'd
Hilda: Can you say more about how that would work, Henry?	Henry's solution needs elaboration to show how it would work in practice.	
Henry: You can only be that princess for one day. Then someone else can be that princess for one day.	Henry explains his idea further. He is dealing with one aspect of the bigger problem the class is working on (i.e., how to keep everyone happy).	
Kathleen: I know. We could sign up every day—like you do for playtime. [Several children nod; a few look unhappy.]	Kathleen has built on Henry's idea and makes actual connections to what she has learned from how the class worked out problems in the past.	
Rhonda: You mean I can't be Cinderella?!	Rhonda has a hard time getting beyond her egocentrism—her own interests and how a solution affects them. This is common with preschoolers.	
Hilda: Rhonda thinks that if we have to sign up she can't be Cinderella when she wants. But we do need to decide on a way children can choose who they'll be and get the roles they like. [She looks at the clock.] It's already past time to go outside. You've been working really hard trying to figure this out. Let's talk about it again tomorrow. We still need to work out what happens with the princes too. And also what things the princesses and princes can do. At outside time, just for today, I've decided there can't be any princesses or princes. [Some of the children groan.] I know some of you don't like that. But it's my job to make sure everyone feels safe outside. I bet by tomorrow we'll figure out a way for that to happen.	Hilda reflects back what Rhonda said without passing judgment, then she restates the problem, giving the specific issue they are currently working on solving. Hilda tries to wind down the discussion. She summarizes and shares her thoughts about other issues for future discussions. She knows that just having such discussions will help the children be more conscious of the princess play and their role in it. Taking seriously her responsibility to keep all children safe, Hilda issues a temporary rule. She thinks banning all princess play for a day will keep children safe and help them clarify their thinking about the role of princesses in their play. Their new understanding can be used in the next day's meeting.	
Haley [Excitedly]: I know! Today we could let everyone be a princess or a prince. Just try for today! [Several children nod in agreement.]	Haley, who has been very invested in the discussion all along because of the trouble she's been having with the play, comes up with her own idea about what the "rule for a day" should be. Her idea grows out of the earlier discussion.	
Hilda: Wow. It looks like a lot of you prefer Haley's solution for today. Well, our rule *is* to find a solution everyone can agree to. So let me try again. Just for today, everyone who wants to can be any princess or prince that they want to be. Tomorrow we'll talk about how it worked and what to do next. [There are a few smiles and nods.]	Hilda shows that she listens to the children and that their voices are important. She uses Haley's solution but still makes it a temporary rule, keeping the children aware of the fact that more work will be done. Changing her mind based on a child's idea helps children experience the power their voices can have.	

Some might argue that Hilda has spent too much time on play issues instead of focusing on basic academic skills. In fact, this effort is closely connected to developing the foundations for learning essential skills. Hilda brings in literacy as she writes down the children's ideas and reads what she wrote back to them as their problem solving continues the next day. This is using reading and writing in context, one of the key ways young children gradually learn how to attach meaning to print. Numeracy is involved as the children think about the concepts of *a lot*, *a few*, and *pairs* of princesses and princes. And as described below, literacy and numeracy will continue to be built into the children's problem-solving efforts.

What's Next?

As the children prepare to go outside, Hilda makes a mental note to herself to carefully observe the children as they engage in princess and prince play to help her figure out how to talk about her observations at the next day's meeting. She also realizes she should try to focus the next discussion on what princesses and princes like to do. She will use this as a time to help expand the current narrow range of activities the children engage in during this play.

She also thinks about how to integrate princess and prince issues into the overall curriculum. As one way to do this, at story time the following day she reads *The Paper Bag Princess* by Robert Munsch, which challenges many of the princess stereotypes that have dominated the children's play. For instance, as Princess Elizabeth is about to marry Prince Ronald, a dragon attacks the castle and kidnaps the prince. Elizabeth disguises herself and cleverly succeeds at rescuing him from the dragon. But Ronald is unsure of how to deal with her unprincess-like behavior.

Not surprisingly, some of the children are indignant. Princesses "don't act or look like that!" they insist. Hilda challenges some of their beliefs with statements such as, "But she *is* a princess and she *does* dress like that . . ." She asks the children, "What do you think would have happened to Prince Ronald if Elizabeth didn't go to rescue him?" and "If you were Princess Elizabeth, what would you do?" As they answer, she once again writes down their responses. She does not correct the children or tell them they're wrong in how they think; rather, she tries to help them problem solve and extend their thinking, as she guides their ideas to be at least a bit less rigid and stereotyped.

Next, Hilda thinks about how to modify the dramatic play area to encourage deeper, more complex play than simply dressing up as princesses and walking around the room going

Box 5.3

Cinderella and Cultural Diversity in the Primary Years

Recognizing that princesses continued to be of high interest to many children beyond kindergarten, one school system added to its second grade curriculum the study of Cinderella stories from a variety of cultures. Teachers and children explore the similarities and differences in the storytelling and characters across cultures, learn literacy skills, and make connections across the curriculum.

Using age-appropriate, culturally diverse books about princesses to help expand children's views and interest in the topic can occur throughout the early childhood years. This can expose children to themes and elements beyond those that are a part of the popular media-inspired renditions many children are familiar with.

to the ball. She works with the children to transform the area into a castle using big blocks as castle walls and strips of foil to create a moat outside the walls. They discuss how to create a drawbridge to get in and out of the castle. In the end they decide to tape big blocks together to make a tall gate that opens and closes. Hilda next helps the children make simple capes by cutting out shiny fabric in several colors and putting small pieces of adhesive Velcro on two corners to attach the capes around their necks. Several children decide to become "super" princes and princesses because they now have "super" capes—thereby incorporating into the play a superhero theme that is of special interest to the boys. And eventually, with Hilda's guidance, the children write their own books about all sorts of princesses and princes who have conventional *and* unconventional adventures. They also work together to make a book about how to make prince and princess adventure capes. The children illustrate some of the books with their own drawings, and they also use photographs of their princess/prince play and creations for illustrations.

ACTION IDEA   Box 5.4

Teachers and Families Working Together

- Share with parents the specific kinds of problems the children are having related to media culture in both their outdoor and indoor play. Include some basic explanations about why you think the problems might be occurring.

- Ask parents whether and how these issues have come up at home and whether parents have any concerns. You can do this through newsletters, during parents' evenings, and at drop-off and pickup times.

- Keep parents informed about your efforts to use their children's interest in specific popular culture media themes, characters, and products to expand, deepen, and transform the children's play and interactions with one another.

- Ask the children's families what they do at home to address these issues. Ask them to suggest ideas that you might use in the classroom.

- Share with parents documentation of the activities you do with children. For example, share books the children have made around a princess theme, or have children take their books home and read them with their families.

- Suggest additional resources—websites, books, guides— that parents can use to help their children get beyond stereotypic or limiting play at home. (Some resources are listed in the Resources section at the end of this book.)

As a result, girls and boys have begun happily playing together, expanding their limited, remote-controlled princess and superhero play. The play keeps evolving and growing, sometimes with Hilda's help and sometimes without. The girls and boys no longer fight over who can be which character from a particular movie, television show, or video game. They continually identify unique problems that they work together to solve in their own unique ways. What a great antidote to problem-solving deficit disorder *and* compassion deficit disorder! Even a great deal of work on literacy gets integrated as the children compose and illustrate new stories about the prince and princess adventures they create.

As you think about how to solve the princess or superhero dilemma—or any other—that may be occurring in your own program, it's important to remember that no class will follow the process exactly as Hilda and the children in her class did. What happened there is unique to this group of children and this particular teacher. It is even highly unlikely that Hilda will re-create the same scenario next year, even if she has a group of children equally involved with princess play, because a new group of children will bring different princess experiences to the classroom and their experiences together will also be different. What happened here evolved from what had previously occurred with princess play, the interests of these particular children, and the skills and prior experiences the children had. Hilda's efforts to scaffold the play in productive ways are based on the lens she developed for understanding and getting beyond remote-controlled childhood.

Whether your class is experiencing the types of issues described in this chapter with princess play or issues that arise from children imitating other popular media-linked characters and scripts, it is helpful to involve parents in the process of identifying and solving the problems. Box 5.4 on page 61 offers some suggestions for doing so (see also Chapter 10). Box 5.5 illustrates one parent's attempts to provide her own young "princess" with some balance. She uses some of the same strategies as Hilda and reaches out to family members and other parents about the issue.

Box 5.5

One Mother and Daughter's Princess Journey

Before her third birthday, Mary's daughter began telling her things like, "Princesses don't run," "They don't wear pants," and "They don't jump because *they're princesses*." Mary found this both strange and disconcerting. How did this 3-year-old, who hadn't been to a child care program or school or seen any princess movies, know all these things? They were facts to the girl. Mary found it odd that she'd built this body of knowledge so quickly and with such certainty. But living with a 3-year-old is often odd, Mary thought, so she chalked it up to a phase.

Most parents Mary talked to told her it *was* a phase, and that it would pass. Parents of girls the same age confirmed that their daughters too were "into the princesses." They said it would go away eventually and to just be patient. But parents of older girls had something different to say. One said, "Be grateful it's just princesses. By kindergarten it will be the latest 'tween star, movie, or television program. Each phase ends and goes into something more upsetting, so be glad it's just Cinderella."

What Did the Mother Do?

• Mary connected with her daughter around her interest in princesses. She asked questions, and her daughter was definite in her answers: Princesses didn't do anything, they certainly didn't run, and they mostly "waited for the prince." Mary observed her daughter's play, and then she began to introduce the idea that princesses could be brave and strong, and that they could leap and run too. Her daughter wasn't buying it, but Mary didn't give up. Slowly, things evolved.

• Mary asked her daughter's grandparents not to buy her princess toys and products or to show her princess movies. She suggested other age-appropriate movies and television programs they could watch with her. When she explained that the princess films would prime Mary's daughter for more meltdowns because there were related products in every grocery store, doctors' office, and major retail store, the grandparents understood.

• Mary began writing a blog about the problem and her solutions (see www.disneyprincessrecovery.blogspot. com). It clearly hit a nerve with other parents—in less than a year it had more than sixty thousand visitors—and she realized she wasn't alone in her struggle to provide her daughter with balance. She learned that the United States is unique in its minimal rules about regulation of marketing to children and that companies can target very young children with little regard for the impact on the children, parents, or wider society.

• As Mary's daughter turned 4 and entered preschool, Mary learned that the teacher had also had to address princesses and other effects of media culture on the children. That year the teacher decided that in place of a Halloween party, the school would host a Harvest Celebration to celebrate fall, costume free. "At Halloween, all the boys dress up as Batman, whacking each other, and the girls come as princesses trying to catch their Batman princes," the teacher told Mary. "It's become too much." Mary commended the teacher for the creative idea of a Harvest Celebration.

Helping Children Get Beyond Remote-Controlled Childhood: Guidelines for Practice

E ducating children in age-appropriate media literacy—the ability to understand, evaluate, and use different types of media—can help them move from being remote controlled to making informed and intentional decisions about their use of screen media, including the television shows they watch, the video and computer games they play, and the apps they use. Although most of the work that has been done so far in media literacy education has involved older children (see, for example, *Media Literacy in the K–12 Classroom*, listed in the Resources section), this chapter will offer suggestions and ideas for developing young children's media literacy.

Media Literacy Skills for Young Children

Information and guidance from the field of media literacy education can help early childhood educators more effectively address both negative and positive ways that media and technology influence young children's development, learning, and behavior. The media literacy field can also provide strategies to help children learn how to

- ◆ Take charge of the screens they use, including the television programs they watch

- ◆ Use tools for understanding the messages the media portray

- ◆ Understand how different forms of media are produced

- ◆ Be more knowledgeable and responsible consumers of media and media-related products to the extent that their level of development allows

Because of how young children think and learn, there are special challenges involved in guiding them to make informed choices. Media literacy develops gradually over time, with maturity, experience, and adult guidance. The more dependent children are on media and the less experience they have had making thoughtful choices, the more help they will need from adults in gaining media literacy. To make an informed choice about which computer or video game to play, television program to watch, or website to visit, a child needs to know what the possibilities are. When selecting a television program, for example, a child needs to know which shows he can watch that are on at that time, which shows are recorded that he can watch at that time, and what will be on each show. A child also needs to be able to consider what the possible consequences of a particular choice are likely to be. Are there shows he will not see if he watches this one? How will he feel or act during or after the show—will it scare him, make him happy? What other activities won't he get to do if he watches television?

Perhaps the biggest challenge to helping children is overcoming the seductive nature of media itself. For instance, when children have a few free minutes or are in transition from one activity to the next, it is often easy and safe to be occupied by something on a screen—seeing whatever is on television or playing a video or computer game. The fast pace and excitement of many screen activities ensures immediate entertainment with little risk or exertion. It can be hard to resist this powerful lure (just as it can for adults many times!), and screen use can quickly become a habit. Turning off a video game, computer, or television presents similar challenges for many children. It can be very hard to make the transition from being passively entertained to actively taking charge of one's activity. One family coined the term "PTVT," or "post-TV trauma," to give legitimacy to this experience and then to figure out what to do to help the children deal with it.

Commercial media programs linked to products aimed at children present an additional challenge. Children's media is designed to get their attention and keep it. Thus, the fast action, dramatic, and often violent scenes get more and more extreme with each popular new show in order to lure children away from the previous popular show. Turning off games or apps can pose similar challenges because there is always "just one more thing" to try to achieve in the play.

In addition, marketing for lines of highly realistic toys and other products linked to children's media results in images from the shows constantly being a part of children's environments. Many children see and hear reminders of media at school and in stores—and therefore, media messages remain on their minds. The high degree to which these images also permeate children's play culture and peer interactions further compounds the difficulty of helping children monitor their responses to media.

Many of the guidelines and strategies introduced here were illustrated in Hilda's efforts to expand the children's focus on princess play in the previous chapter. You can use these strategies to help children get beyond remote-controlled childhood in meaningful and unique ways—to connect with children to help them disconnect. The more you succeed at helping children use appropriate media now and to take more initiative in their own play experiences, the better equipped they will be to learn to make choices about screen use in the future. The chapters that follow will describe and illustrate the strategies in greater depth.

What You Can Do: Considering and Counteracting Negative Media Influences

While traditional media literacy efforts focus primarily on helping children learn to understand, evaluate, and use different forms of media, *Beyond Remote-Controlled Childhood* takes a broader approach. That is, throughout this book, we look at how you can help children deal with the range of ways media and media culture affect them, and how you can promote the positive effects and counteract the negative ones. I often call this "media education" rather than "media literacy."

Promote Child-Controlled Activities

As we saw in Chapter 3, media and media culture can have a harmful impact on *process issues*—that is, issues related to how children learn from and interact in the real world. To help counter this, teachers can promote *child-controlled* activities and ideas instead of *remote-controlled* activities and ideas that are influenced by the media children are exposed to. As children try to imitate and replicate characters, images, and stories they get from the media, help them bring in their own ideas and actions so that they—not the script writers of television shows, video games, and apps—can gradually be the creators of what happens. In Chapter 5, we saw Hilda doing this in many ways as the children came up with new rules for guiding their princess play, created costumes and a block castle, and wrote prince and princess stories.

Encourage Problem Finding and Problem Solving

Most aspects of early childhood classroom life can provide opportunities for children to build problem-finding and problem-solving skills. When children see themselves as problem finders and problem solvers—who can figure out how to make a block tower taller and taller without it falling down, for example—they develop curiosity about their world and confidence in their ability to figure things out for themselves. Solving one problem leads to a new problem, which they solve by using the skills they developed from solving previous problems. In the course of playing this way, children develop deep interests as they improve and eventually become "experts" at problem solving. This process of identifying and solving problems provides an important antidote to problem-solving deficit disorder, as well as a powerful foundation for helping children become motivated, competent learners who are actively engaged with their environment in school and in life (Levin 2007).

Media literacy develops gradually over time, with maturity, experience, and adult guidance.

However, many children's involvement with media and media culture can channel them into someone else's script, thus limiting their opportunities to find and solve their own problems. Help children identify interesting problems to solve. Take them step by step through the process of defining the issue or situation and looking for solutions. Let them try out their solutions to see how they work. This process will diminish what can be described as problem-solving deficit disorder, which was discussed in Chapter 3. Hilda's problem-solving discussions with the children about how to deal with conflicts on the playground illustrate how this process can work.

Support the Development of Caring Relationships and Peaceful Conflict Resolution

There are many ways to build relationships among children in the classroom, thereby providing an antidote to compassion deficit disorder. You can include the topic in class discussions, plan activities where children learn together, use stressful situations as an opportunity to examine cause and effect, and encourage children to take another's point of view. All of these approaches can help counteract negative lessons about relationships that children sometimes pick up through the media.

There are signs of compassion deficit disorder among children in the discussion of princess play in the previous chapter. Hilda was very concerned about how mean-spirited behavior seemed to be escalating in the play. Because of their egocentric thinking, children focused on the one thing they cared about most in the heat of the moment and had difficulty thinking about the impact of their actions on others. Hilda made relationships a central part of what she worked on in her discussions with the children.

Value and Facilitate Creative, Child-Centered Play

As discussed in Part One, many children play less at home today, in part because of the time they spend engaged with screens. As a result, they may have trouble coming up with their own creative play ideas when they play with others, which I call play deficit disorder. They often need adult assistance to learn how to engage in the kind of play that contributes to becoming active, engaged skill-builders and learners.

The play of some of the children in Hilda's class, especially before she gets involved in facilitating it, shows qualities that are part of play deficit disorder. The children focus so much on trying to replicate the highlights of what they have learned about princesses from media that they do not seem to be able to get very far with creating actual play scenarios. This is one key reason Hilda uses the second meeting to encourage the children to come up with ideas about how to take control of and expand their princess play into something of their own making. She hopes that as the play itself becomes more complex and child created it will counteract the problems of play deficit disorder. (Strategies for facilitating play in today's screen-saturated world are discussed at length in Chapter 7).

Consider the Developmental Level of the Children

When working to counteract harmful aspects of media culture in young children's lives, it is rarely effective to simply tell children how to think about and respond to media messages. They are not yet fully logical thinkers and have a hard time making logical-causal connections. Young children deal with concrete information, not abstract ideas. They need to make their own unique connections in their own ways about what you are trying to teach. Thus, the more you can engage in hands-on, child-centered, give-and-take discussions and activities with children around media issues, the more impact you are likely to have on their development, understanding, and behavior. (For more information about how children's thinking affects the impact media has on them, see Chapters 2 and 8.)

As described in Chapter 5, Hilda's discussion with the children follows a six-step process to help them problem solve and suggest possible solutions. This child-centered problem-solving process, which is adapted from the adult field of conflict resolution (Fisher, Ury, & Patton 2011; Levin 2003), provides a very helpful framework for working on meaningful issues with groups of children and for addressing individual conflicts. It also can be used to facilitate and expand children's play. Thus, it is a useful tool for addressing aspects of problem-solving deficit disorder, compassion deficit disorder, and play deficit disorder. This six-step process is outlined in Box 6.1.

Help Children Connect What They Learn From the Real World and the World of Screens

Create structures and routines that allow media-related conversations to happen when you can be directly involved rather than just letting children discuss it among themselves. Help children know that it is safe to bring up whatever media issues are on their minds. Many children have learned that adults aren't interested in, or get upset with, what they say about media. As you talk to children about the media, help them use what they

---

Box 6.1

Six-Step Problem-Solving Process

Help children do the following:

1. Learn to see and understand the problem.

Understanding the problem is an essential first step in thinking about what kinds of actions might solve it. Because of how young children think, it can be hard for them to put the pieces of a problem together into a meaningful whole. They often need help identifying and understanding problems. Part of this step is acknowledging the thoughts and feelings of the children involved so that they feel understood and validated by the adult.

2. Help children identify possible solutions and explore how each idea might solve the problem.

Generating a range of ideas for solving a problem involves trying to make logical cause-and-effect connections, which is difficult for young children. This means that they will come up with many ideas that you know probably won't work. But that's okay because of the next step!

3. Figure out how each possible solution might work in practice.

Because young children tend to focus on one thing at a time and have difficulty imagining what they cannot see, they can have a hard time visualizing how a solution will work before trying it out. Helping children talk through the concrete actions involved with possible solutions puts them in a much better position to make an informed choice and to implement it.

4. Choose a solution everyone can agree to try.

The goal here is to find a win-win solution that the children have ideas about putting into practice and that ensures all children involved feel their points of view have been heard and respected. It is important that the solution not be one that the teacher imposes on the children but one they all agree to try.

5. Put the solution into practice.

Children often need help figuring out how to get started, as they coordinate their own actions with the other children involved and identify the effects of those actions.

6. Evaluate how the solution worked and how to make it work better.

This helps children learn that problem solving is part of an ongoing process in which mistakes are okay and that they can improve at finding effective solutions.

---

know from their family–school–societal culture box (as described in Chapter 3) to interpret the messages—both positive and negative—that they get from the media culture box. Hilda used this strategy to help the children who tended to focus on how princesses look and what they should and should not do channel their activities into more prosocial, creative play.

Lead Group Discussions About Media-Related Topics

Group discussions, like the ones about princesses presented in Chapter 5, provide a powerful way for connecting with children around the things they care about most, which have a big influence on their ideas and behavior. Such conversations also allow children to hear and discuss their classmates' responses and to learn that there can be a wide range of possible feelings and thoughts related to a topic. This exposure to diverse ideas can help children consider new possibilities for themselves. While no two conversations will ever be the same, Hilda's efforts to use the children's interest in princesses as a way to gain information and build children's skills provide an excellent example of what to aim for.

As you saw in the discussions in Chapter 5, leading give-and-take conversations with children about media-related issues can be a challenge. There rarely is one right way to do it. It takes practice and a willingness to take risks and be comfortable with not knowing where a discussion might lead. The princess and prince discussions illustrate how having goals and starting questions in mind can provide structure. At the same time, you need to be ready to scaffold a meaningful discussion with children based on what they say. Other give-and-take discussions in this book provide additional examples of how to do this. When leading give-and-take discussions with children, keep the following strategies and goals in mind:

♦ **Create an atmosphere where it feels safe to express diverse ideas.** To discuss, think through, and work out media issues in a meaningful way, children need to feel safe saying what they really think. Otherwise they may parrot what they think adults want to hear or just stay out of the discussion. In a safe atmosphere, children are likely to honestly reflect on and develop new strategies and approaches for thinking about the issues being discussed (the *real* goal for such discussions).

♦ **Help children put their ideas into words and share them with others through give-and-take dialogues.** Expressing their ideas in a way others can understand is a skill young children are just developing. To assist them with this, restate what children say, filling in to make the meaning clearer.

For example, if a child says, "The Power Rangers hurt me," you might say, "You mean when you were outside and some children were playing Power Rangers, they hurt you with a karate chop?" Or, if a child says, "I don't hurt," you might say, "Do you mean when you play Power Ranger games you don't karate chop anyone?" This helps all the children understand what is being said and helps them follow the discussion.

◆ **Ask open-ended questions that have many possible answers, and respect the diverse ways children respond.** A goal for this kind of discussion is to help children gradually learn to be critical viewers of television and responsible media users. Answering questions that don't have one right answer and hearing others' answers to the questions is one way children build up a database of understanding. Box 6.2 on page 68 provides open-ended questions that will help you get started. Try to come up with follow-up questions to help children expand on what they say.

◆ **Communicate that there can be many possible answers.** Don't focus on what you feel are right or wrong answers. Help children explore the possible answers in ways they can understand and see how they connect to their own ideas and behaviors.

◆ **Ask questions and bring in information or ideas that complicate children's thinking.** One effective way to help children learn new ideas is to introduce ideas that *challenge* in a nonjudgmental way—not put down or "correct"—their thinking. For example, if children say that their television-linked fighting play is "only pretend," their teacher might point out that "Even when it's pretend, some children are *really* getting hurt." This can lead to more discussion about what is pretend and what is real, as well as how to pretend without hurting others.

◆ **When possible, end discussions with a concrete plan of action.** By generating some concrete ideas about what to do, children learn how to put words into action, explore issues further, solve problems, and change their behavior—crucial steps in counteracting problem-solving and compassion deficit disorder and turning remote-controlled behavior into self-generated behavior. Ending a discussion this way also communicates to children that they have the power to make an impact and to change things.

Box 6.5 on page 70 shows comments from a class discussion about what the children were seeing in the media and what they thought about it. This example is from several years ago, but the lessons

---

ACTION IDEA — Box 6.3

Media Surveys for Children Who Can Read and Write

Have children survey classmates about media-related issues. Begin with a meeting to come up with questions to ask. Individual children or groups of children can each have a question to survey. Then have a meeting to share and discuss what the children discovered. The children can also graph their results.

ACTION IDEA — Box 6.4

Recording Discussions

When you have conversations with children about media issues, record the discussions in a way that does not divert the children's interest from the discussion to the technology being used for recording. Later, listen to the recordings to reflect on how the discussion went, what you learned from the children, and what they learned from you. Were there questions you wish you had asked but didn't, or things you wish you had said differently? Use this information to help you develop ideas about how to proceed.

Class Discussion of Scary Things Seen on Screens

During a discussion between 5- to 7-year-olds and their teachers about the media programming the children were allowed and were not allowed to watch in their homes, one child mentioned a show that she wished she had not seen. The children ended up discussing the question "Have you ever watched anything you wish you hadn't?" Here is a summary of the children's responses. Most of the episodes they describe occurred when the children were younger.

- My brother gets really scared by movies and then he says he isn't. My parents are really careful about what we can watch.

- When I was little, I saw *It* on TV about a clown who eats people. I wanted to watch because it was about a clown. I got really scared. I still have the pictures in my head. I didn't tell anyone because I *snuck*.

- Dad rented *Ghostbusters*. I had nightmares for a whole year. I was worried the ghosts would burst through the walls and kill me. Mom got mad.

- I saw *Robocops* and close-ups of *Jaws*. The guy got shot 30 times. I kept thinking about it when I was going to sleep.

- I saw *Cape Fear*. It has a guy who kills a dog. He got drunk. He took this woman home and handcuffed her to the bed and bit her. It wasn't scary. Just disgusting. I saw it at my friend's house. Her mom lets her see lots of disgusting stuff.

- We saw *Treasure Island*. I kept going in and out of the room 'cuz I got so scared.

- When I was younger I saw a show—I can't remember the name—that had a lot of guns and people getting shot. I worried I was going to be murdered like that.

- I was really scared by a skeleton they had on *Sesame Street* that moved.

- I used to watch the news with my dad. It really freaked me out because of all the people who break into your house. I have this back door and worried that people would come in.

- When I was really small, *Bambi* got me really sad when the mother got killed. I remember going to my mom's bed at night.

- I [a boy] was really embarrassed when I saw *Bambi*. I was really scared and cried and my friend didn't.

we can learn from it are still relevant today. These responses poignantly reveal that children may see a wide range of programming in the media that many adults would consider inappropriate for them. The comments clearly illustrate how using the guidelines outlined previously can lead to rich and meaningful discussions that deeply reflect children's understanding and concerns. Through such discussions, children are able to talk about important experiences that they often must handle on their own. In addition, teachers learn so much about the children—the diverse ways in which screen content affects children's thoughts, feelings, and behaviors, and how children's reactions are not always predictable. For example, programming generally considered appropriate for their age group distressed some of the children. Finally, these reactions illustrate why it is so important for adults to stay connected and establish a dialogue with children about the media in their lives—so that children have a safe way to talk about it and feel supported.

Help Children Learn More About Media

Engage children in learning about how television programs and other media are made. Given how young children think, it can be hard for them to figure out how what they see on screens is the same and different from what they actually experience in life. Learning more about the various parts of media and how they work is a good starting point for understanding how media differs from real life. It can also help turn what can often be the more passive consumption of someone else's media program into more active thinking, doing, and learning.

Record and Experiment With Sound Effects

Have children record a variety of sounds. They can play them back and decide what they sound like, play guessing games with their sounds, write their own stories to go with the sounds, and make and record their own sounds to accompany a segment of a television program, movie, or video.

Introduce Flip Books

Use flip books to help children explore animation and cartoons. You can purchase simple ones; older children can make their own books.

Help Children Explore the Media Production Process

◆ Encourage children to write scripts with words and pictures. Often this works best with especially interesting experiences the children have had themselves or know about.

◆ Have children rewrite familiar and popular scripts to make them more warmhearted, inclusive, and peaceful, or to give them happier endings. Children often also enjoy informally acting out their scripts.

◆ Film the children's productions using a camera, phone, or tablet. They can revise their productions and try to bring in special effects and sounds. Filming very simple sequences of action planned by the children can also produce interesting results. It helps the children better understand how some of the things they see on the screen are actually created.

◆ Examine media production techniques using taped segments of children's programs (including those from discussions you may have had about media issues such as violence and what is pretend and real). For example, if children start talking about some amazing or violent thing they saw a character do in a film or television program, try to find an example of the character doing what the children saw, watch it, and have a discussion about how the "amazing" thing might have happened or what the character could have done besides hurting people.

◆ Play just the audio part of a small segment of a taped program. Ask the children to guess what they think is happening in the picture.

◆ Show the visual part of the tape without the sound. Ask the children to predict what the sound will be like. Have them compose their own sounds.

◆ Record and show an episode of a television show the children like to watch. Choose a few segments that use special effects to make fantastic or impossible things happen, and ask the children to try to figure out how it was made. They don't have to come up with one right answer; the goal here is to teach them the tools for beginning to think critically about media when they are viewing a program and afterward.

Help Children Learn to Take Charge of Their Screen Time

Building on the information obtained from the children's media surveys (see Box 6.3 on page 69) and through your conversations with children, you can begin discussions and develop activities that get children focused on making conscious choices about television programs, movies, computer games, apps, and other screen technologies. It is important to involve families in these efforts. Let them know what is happening in the classroom related to the children and media and why you are addressing the topic by sharing the results of the children's media survey and through newsletters, notes home, and other communication channels. Work with parents to learn how they use media at home and whether they have concerns about their children's usage. (See Chapter 4 for a parent letter and survey. Chapter 10 contains many additional suggestions for working with families.)

Any group of children, or adults, will have a range of opinions about what is good and bad about media and what is okay to watch or use and what is not. When children express differing ideas or disagree about the appropriateness of a media choice, help them explore the issues that may underlie the disagreement. The more active the role children play in making decisions about what to watch or use, the more meaningful and effective those choices are likely to be. Remember to connect with families so they can support these efforts in ways that work in their homes. (See Chapter 10 for some specific ways you can do this.) While many of the examples shown in the boxes on the next several pages are related to television viewing, they can easily be adapted for other kinds of screen usage.

Include All Types of Screen Devices in the Discussion

Numerous types of screen activities are available today that can consume children's time. In many cases, screen time gradually becomes a greater and greater part of children's lives without much awareness that time spent in real-world activities is slowly decreasing. Thus, when considering with children how much and what media they will consume, it is important to include all screen activities in the discussion—watching television programs and videos, playing computer or video games, using apps on smartphones or tablets, visiting websites, etc.—and to help children decide how to include nonscreen activities in their lives.

Develop Guidelines With Children for Limiting Screen Time

How much screen time children are allowed to engage in will vary from family to family. The American Academy of Pediatrics (AAP; 2012) suggests no more than an hour or two a day of entertainment screen time for children older than 2 years. Whatever the time limit families have set, an overall goal is to help children keep

---

ACTION IDEA   Box 6.6

Encourage Children to Keep Screen Diaries

Provide paper and other materials so children can make their own screen diaries about what programs, games, apps, and so on they plan to watch or use. Later they can note what they did watch or use.

Variations and Extensions

• Children with differing levels of reading and writing skills can keep their screen diaries in different ways. Prereaders and early readers can draw pictures to represent, for example, each show they plan to watch and then circle them after the show; you can help write down program names and other information. Older children can add additional details such as a schedule of days and times and/or a sentence or two about what they saw or did.

• Lead individual or group discussions about the content of children's screen diaries on a regular basis: "How did your planning work? What was hard about it? What worked well? What would you like to change about your planning? What do your parents say about screen time?"

• Through such discussions, children can learn about the screen time practices of their classmates. They may come up with ideas for changing when and what they watch or use and for expanding the information they keep in their screen diaries. The goal here is for children to become more self-aware of the process of making informed screen choices and to have more tools for accomplishing this. As they do this, they may hear about how other children do things that they want to do too—for instance, spend more time with screens or see shows their parents have banned. When this happens, it is important to point out to the children that families make different choices. The process won't always be easy, and stressors may arise. This is another reason it is important to collaborate with parents, so they know something about the origins of these issues if they arise at home.

---

their television viewing and other screen time at a level low enough that they do not become dependent on these activities to fill their time. In most cases, this will mean that less is better.

Talk with children about their families' viewing guidelines and limits, and make a list of them together. Why have parents set the rules? How are they fair? How not? Invite children to express their own ideas about what the guidelines should be. Because young children are still gradually developing an understanding of time, they will need your assistance. Often, the number of shows or games and the times of day to watch or play are the kinds of units children can discuss meaningfully.

Share the children's discussion with their families by helping children write a letter home that allows them to tell their parents what screen rules they think are fair. Offer art materials so children can make pictures about screen time rules—the ones they have at home or the ones they think would be good. In many cases, letting parents know their children's ideas and feelings can pave the way for meaningful discussions and collaborative media rule making between children and parents—helping them decide together what and when they will watch.

Help Children Reduce Their Dependence on Screens

A vital part of helping children successfully limit their screen time is making sure they have appealing alternative activities. Be aware that often the more time children spend with screens, the harder it is for them to take charge of and limit their screen time. Guide children in identifying appealing activities to do instead of using screens. A key to achieving success here is helping children plan a range of activities that capture their interest, meet their needs, build on their skills, and are inherently satisfying. Because it is easy to turn on the television, a video game, or some other screen device on impulse, help children learn how to plan in advance for other activities they can do when they have some free time.

Box 6.7

Plan for Screen Viewing for _____

Even before learning to read and write, children can make a Plan for Screen Viewing by drawing pictures of the shows, programs, or games they pan to watch or use. Adults can help write down names and times. Here is an example of a plan you might use with children.

Day of week	Picture of Activity #1	Picture of Activity #2	Picture of Activity #3
_____	Name_____ When_____	Name_____ When_____	Name_____ When_____
_____	Name_____ When_____	Name_____ When_____	Name_____ When_____

TV Rules We Have at Home

This chart was generated by kindergartners at the beginning of a discussion of their ideas about television rules. In a follow-up activity they wrote letters to their parents about television rules. In later discussions and activities, they discussed rules for other kinds of screen activities.

- No TV before school
- No TV after dinner
- No TV during dinner
- Nobody can sit too close to the TV
- No fighting over the best TV chair
- TV on weekends only
- No turning the channel when someone else is watching
- The TV can only be on until 8:30 at night
- You can't turn on the TV just because you're bored
- No blocking anybody else
- Only two shows a day
- No TV that's really scary
- We don't have any rules (three children)

Dear _____,

Today in school we talked about TV rules. I think we should have some TV rules in our house. Here is my idea:

Love,

Share Relevant Children's Books

As a starting point for discussing screen-free activities, share some children's books that address screen issues (see Box 6.11 on page 77). Ask the children what they would do if they found themselves in the same situation as the characters in the book—the television broke, the power went out, or some other event prevented them from using screens. Make a list or chart (with illustrations, especially for nonreaders) of children's ideas.

Generate Ideas for Free-Time Activities

Post a chart with ideas for free-time activities in a central place in the classroom. Add children's new activity ideas to the list throughout the year. Periodically lead a discussion about what screen-free activities children did over the previous weekend (or the day before). List children's responses and ask them to brainstorm other things they could have done. Ask older children to keep diaries of what they do with their out-of-school time. Ask them to record both screen and nonscreen time. Then they can make simple graphs showing their data.

Share Ideas With Families

Send home a list of free-time activity ideas with a note for families, or post the ideas on the class's blog or website. Encourage parents to talk with their children about the ideas on the list and work together to develop the alternative activities of most interest that are likely to work for their household. Ask parents to send in their own family's additions for the list.

Encourage Children to Teach One Another About Activities

Children can share their special skills and interests. Set up a system for children to teach one another about activities. Establish a regular time for sharing, and post a sign-up sheet so children can plan for their turn to share. Note that this way of working with other children can be a very meaningful and age-appropriate way to learn to take the perspective of another, thereby helping to counteract compassion deficit disorder.

Box 6.9

Children's Television Rule Pictures

Here are some examples of pictures about television viewing rules made by kindergartners to share with their families. The teacher also made a book of the children's television rules to place in the classroom library. The children's rules provide a window into what they learned from class discussions. For example, the child who suggested the rule "No watching on sunny days" seems to realize that on pleasant days children could play outside instead of staying inside with a screen.

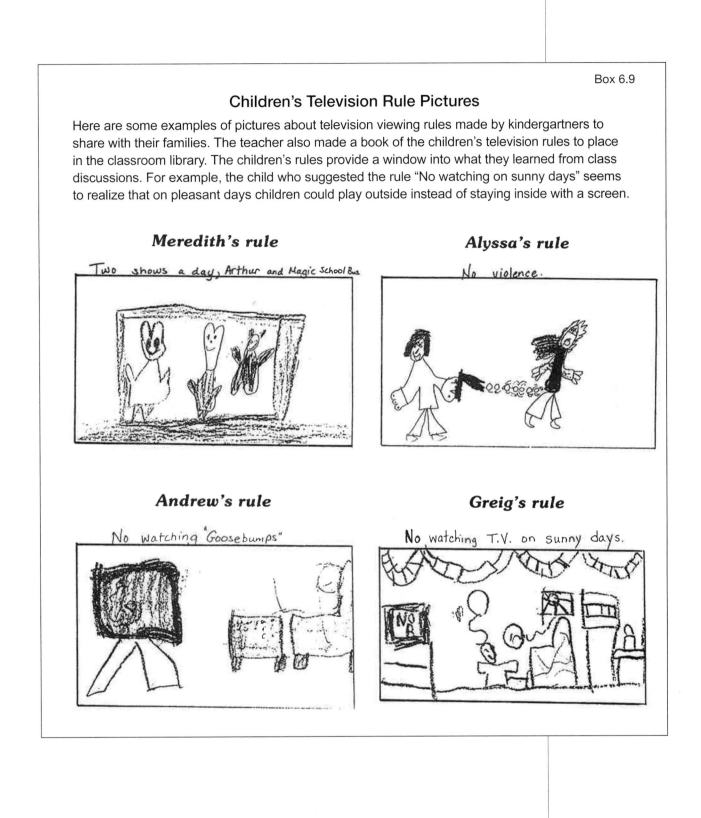

Meredith's rule

Two shows a day, Arthur and Magic School Bus

Alyssa's rule

No violence.

Andrew's rule

No watching "Goosebumps"

Greig's rule

No watching T.V. on sunny days.

Box 6.10

Second-Graders' Letters to Parents About TV Rules

Dear family

In school we have been learning about kids and TV. Now that it's Turn Off The TV Week, we're talking about the TV rules we have in our homes. I think we should have the following TV rules in our house:

1. no talking wen the t.v. is on.

2. no standing in front of the t.v.

3. no violent shows.

Let's talk about these ideas as a family so we can have TV rules we all agree on!

Love, Cory

Second-graders wrote letters to their parents about television rules. These letters illustrate how activities suggested in this book can be adapted for children of different ages and skill levels.

Dear mom and Dad

In school we have been learning about kids and TV. Now that it's Turn Off The TV Week, we're talking about the TV rules we have in our homes. I think we should have the following TV rules in our house:

1. no soup operas

2. make a limit for T.V.

3. no woching moves thetor radio

Let's talk about these ideas as a family so we can have TV rules we all agree on!

Love, Kimberly

ACTION IDEA

Box 6.11

What Would You Do If the Televison Broke?

Read the book *Mouse TV* by Matt Novak. Although written some years ago, its message is still relevant to today's children. The story is about the anxiety a family of mice experience when their television set breaks down and how they solve the problem of being without it. If *Mouse TV* or a similar book is not available, present a "Pretend your television set broke . . ." scenario and invite the children to respond.

Children Discuss the Book

One kindergarten teacher read this book aloud and then helped the children make a chart of all their suggestions about what the mice could do instead of watching television. She wrote down all of their ideas, even if they didn't exactly relate to the question or contribute in an obvious way to the discussion. Here are their responses. They can:

Fix it	Read books	Play on the swings
Get a new TV	Eat fruit	Ride bikes
Go upstairs in their	Build things with a hammer	Play with toys
room and play a game	Play in the sandbox	Play with dolls
Exchange the TV	Play LEGOs	Draw a picture
Maybe the volume is broken	Play soccer	Play with blocks

After making this list, the kindergartners each drew a picture of a favorite idea and combined them into a big book to go into their class library.

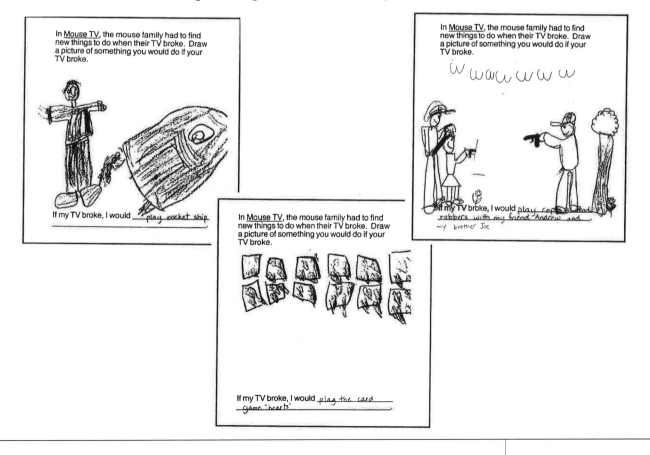

Box 6.11 cont'd

Four-year-olds drew what they thought the mouse family could do after their television broke.

Box 6.12

Children's Drawings of Ideas for TV-Free Day
or Weekend Activities

During their school's special TV-Free Week, children made drawings of activities they could do instead of watching television. To the teacher's surprise, many of the children simply turned to other forms of screen time, such as video games, videos, and computers.

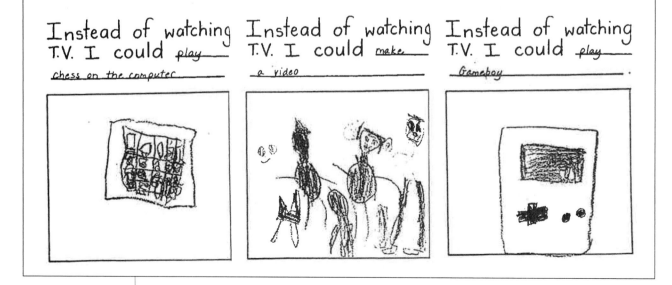

Box 6.13

Children Teaching Children Sign-Up Sheet

This sign-up sheet allowed kindergartners in one class to learn new activities and cut down on their screen time. The teacher inserted simple illustrations so both readers and nonreaders could understand the chart. Throughout the year, as children learned new things to share with classmates, the teacher added and removed activities from the sheet. Periodically during class meetings the teacher and children discussed how they had helped their classmates and suggested additional ways to be helpful.

The Teacher	I Can Teach	I Want To Learn
Melanie	Checkers	1. _____ 2. _____ 3. _____
Jason	Bubble blowing	1. _____ 2. _____ 3. _____
Prita	Hard puzzles	1. _____ 2. _____ 3. _____
Julie & Deon	LEGO marble ramps	1. _____ 2. _____ 3. _____
Arthur	Drawing action figures	1. _____ 2. _____ 3. _____
Amena	Cat's cradle	1. _____ 2. _____ 3. _____

The Value of Helping Children Get Beyond Remote-Controlled Childhood in Today's Educational Climate

You may well be wondering how you can possibly fit any of the many activities suggested here into your busy classroom schedule. This can be a challenge given the curriculum and early learning standards you are already addressing, especially as the demands on teachers have increased.

However, as we will discuss more fully in the next two chapters, counteracting the negative effects that can result from media and screen usage—both the process and the content influences—is likely to provide children with a better foundation for learning and enable them to become more engaged in learning. I have worked with many teachers to help them assist children to gain control of their own activities. They often voice relief when, after an infusion of activities similar to those discussed in this book, they find the children have gained the skills needed to actively engage in all aspects of the learning process. This actually can make *all* aspects of teaching easier.

These experiences make me wonder if the growing focus of early childhood policy on teaching basic skills is related to the observation that children today seem to learn differently from children in the past. Perhaps they are not as engaged in an active learning process because of how media and media culture are affecting both how they learn and what they are interested in learning. If this is the case, teaching remote-controlled children with remote-controlled drill-and-practice lessons, as many school reforms seem to embrace, will only perpetuate the problem. It will not help children learn how to become actively engaged in the learning and meaning-making process. If we truly want to help children become effective learners, we must develop strategies that take into account the impact of remote-controlled childhood. We must help them become engaged learners and critical thinkers. (For more information on this, visit the Defending the Early Years project website: www.dey project.org.)

All of the activities proposed here, in addition to helping teachers counteract remote-controlled childhood, provide rich and meaningful ways to work on language, reading and writing, math, and science. Understanding the connections between media activities and more standard curriculum content and subject areas can enhance how you cover the required curriculum and can help you document the impact of the media activities you do.

The curriculum web on producing a "television show" shown in Box 6.17 on page 82 illustrates connections between the suggested activities and subject areas in many curricula. You can make webs like this when planning specific media activities to help you work out in a purposeful manner how to connect the activity to other aspects of children's learning.

ACTION IDEA Box 6.16

A Special Screen-Free Week Activity:
Ask Children to Keep an Activity Log

During Screen-Free Week, encourage children to write down what they do instead of using screens. Here is an example of a screen-free activity log kept by a third-grader in a Boston public school.

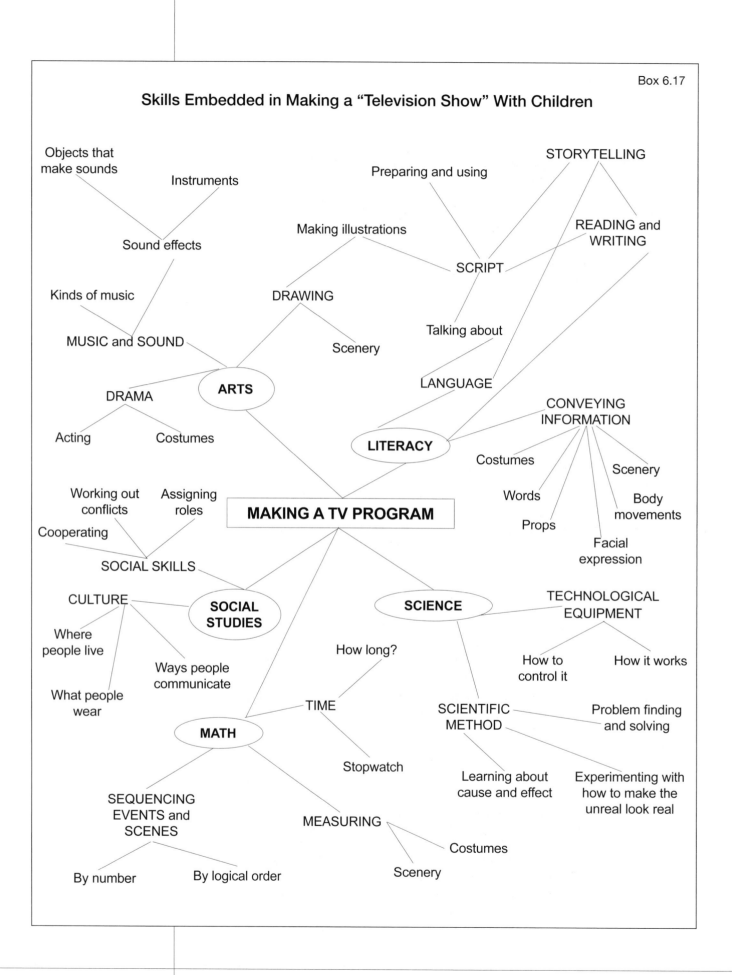

Skills Embedded in Making a "Television Show" With Children

Box 6.17

Objects that make sounds

Instruments

Sound effects

Kinds of music

MUSIC and SOUND

DRAMA

Acting   Costumes

Making illustrations

DRAWING

Scenery

ARTS

STORYTELLING

Preparing and using

READING and WRITING

SCRIPT

Talking about

LANGUAGE

LITERACY

CONVEYING INFORMATION

Costumes   Scenery

Words   Body movements

Props

Facial expression

Working out conflicts   Assigning roles

Cooperating

SOCIAL SKILLS

MAKING A TV PROGRAM

CULTURE

Where people live

What people wear

Ways people communicate

SOCIAL STUDIES

SCIENCE

TECHNOLOGICAL EQUIPMENT

How to control it   How it works

How long?

TIME

Stopwatch

MATH

SCIENTIFIC METHOD

Problem finding and solving

Learning about cause and effect

Experimenting with how to make the unreal look real

SEQUENCING EVENTS and SCENES

MEASURING

Costumes

By number   By logical order

Scenery

Beyond Remote-Controlled Play: Helping Children Become Creative Players

Four-year-old Jason, a child in Janelle's class, talks about Batman all day long. He dissolves into tears one day upon learning that there is no more masking tape. Without masking tape, he does not know how to make himself a "power shooter"—a wristband that he likes to wear "just like Batman wears." He cries, "Then I won't have powers!" This prop seems critical for him to know how to play. For many days in a row, he has made himself a power shooter and played Batman. Figuring out how to make this prop required considerable creative thinking and problem solving, but once he created it, his play became repetitive and focused on running, hiding, and shooting. With no tape to make his prop, Jason seems to be at a loss about how and what to play, despite having been introduced to a full range of engaging materials available in the classroom. Janelle talks with Jason about other ways to make a wristband, but Jason seems unwilling or unable to consider a different way of creating one.

*   *   *

Sasha, almost 3 years old, has recently begun to pretend and uses this vital skill over and over again in her play with her favorite stuffed animal, "Hoppi" (that's *hippo* with the vowels switched). She often uses a high-pitched voice to ask Hoppi questions, and she shares with him everything she does. For example, she pretends to offer Hoppi a snack when she has one.

One day, Sasha asks her caregiver if she can turn on the television. When her request is turned down, she makes a big frown and goes over to Hoppi. She asks him if he would like to watch *Thomas & Friends*. Her caregiver is a bit concerned that a power struggle about turning on the television is about to occur, but instead, Sasha sits on the couch with Hoppi and watches the blank screen. She starts giving Hoppi a play-by-play account of her version of a *Winnie the Pooh* episode. "Look, Hoppi. Pooh is flying! Do you see he wants some honey?" Soon she puts her finger in the air to "switches channels" to *Sesame Street.* Now she starts to explain counting to Hoppi. "Listen, Hoppi . . . 1-2-3-4-5-6-7, like that. Can you count too? Big Bird can help you count!"

The Importance of Play in Development, Learning, and School Success

Play is central to all aspects of young children's healthy development and learning, including the foundations they need for successfully mastering academic skills as they get older. (For an in-depth analysis and discussion of the central role of play in children's development and learning, read *Play at the Center of the Curriculum* by J. Van Hoorn, P. Nourot, B. Scales, and K. Alward. This book is listed in the Resources section.) To fully understand the central role of play, we need to look at both the *nature and quality of the play process* as well as *what children learn* as they play. Children actively use play to try out new ideas and situations and to master skills and experiences—including what they see on screens. In the process, they build new ideas and skills. They also learn how to find interesting problems to work on and how to solve those problems in creative ways. And when they do, they often experience a sense of inner power and competence that can come from actively working things out on their own. They learn, "I can do it!" This becomes a strong motivator for further exploration and learning.

The more children's play is a creation of their prior experiences, imagination, abilities, and needs, the more fully it will contribute to their social, emotional, and intellectual development and learning. That is, when children are in control of what happens and work on solving their own problems in their play—as scriptwriters, actors, prop people, producers, and directors—they are most likely to get the full benefits of play. And because children are unique individuals bringing different experiences and understandings to their play, each child's play will be unique. (For more on the rationale for fantasy play, see *The Case for Make Believe: Saving Play in a Commercialized World* by S. Linn, listed in the Resources section).

In the vignette above about Sasha, we see her doing these things in her television-"watching" play with Hoppi as she encounters a problem (she cannot watch television) and devises a meaningful and satisfying way to solve the problem (by creating her own television script). Her solution draws on her prior experience with and understanding of particular television programs, using those parts of the shows that are most meaningful to her. Because she knows how to play on her own and create her own play "scripts," she is able to deal with the frustration of not being able to turn on the television and to transform it into a learning experience. Her play illustrates the process of problem solving and meaning making described in earlier chapters that is an essential part of all effective learning for young children.

As we observe her play, we learn a lot about Sasha and her level of development, skills, and interests that could help us plan appropriate play and learning activities for her. She knows how to pretend that objects exist when they don't and can represent real experiences through pretend actions. Both of these skills are vital precursors to reading. For instance, Sasha will come to learn that what look like squiggles on a paper represent letters that, when combined in certain sequences, stand for sounds and words. She is interested in trying out what she knows about counting and can use numbers in sequence (even though we would probably not yet expect her to understand one-to-one correspondence and be able to connect one object to each number). We also learn that Sasha is able to bring the content of television programs she sees into her play to work out its meaning and to develop skills. Her play, although based upon her screen experiences, is not remote controlled; it is a unique creation that continues to evolve as she plays.

Jason's play, however, tells a different story. Jason has one idea in mind (Batman play) that comes directly out of what he has seen Batman do (use a wristband to send out powerful forces). He worked out the problem of how to play Batman some time ago by figuring out how to use tape to make his own Batman wristbands. But on this day he feels that if he cannot make the wristbands, then he cannot play. And even when he is able to make his wristbands, his play is repetitive; he uses the violent wristband action over and over without building on this action to extend his play. He appears unable to find new interesting problems to work on or to bring in new skills and ideas to master. He is stuck, and his ability to learn through his play is compromised. (For a more in-depth discussion about how media violence affects play with violent themes, see *The War Play Dilemma* by D. Levin and N. Carlsson-Paige, listed in the Resources section.)

The account of Jason's play is very much like the descriptions I hear over and over from teachers who struggle to address media-based play in their programs. For some boys, such play is usually based on superheroes from television shows and movies. For some girls, it's the latest teen star or glamorized doll. Teachers often describe this media-scripted play as repetitive and similar to the play of all the other children who engage in it. When children do begin an open-ended play activity, teachers report, many soon say they are bored, and they rarely get deeply involved in the play or take charge of shaping their play as Sasha did. These are typical characteristics of play deficit disorder.

The differences in how Jason and Sasha deal with their media-related frustrations illustrate an important barometer for judging the extent to which media can impede children's play and development. We might reasonably be concerned about Jason and his screen use. Based on the information given here, he seems to be controlled by what he has seen on screens and cannot get beyond it to create his own play that will promote his learning and development. In contrast, there does not seem to be cause for concern about Sasha's screen use because she is able to bring what she knows about screens into her rich and meaningful play without the screens controlling it. She is capable of using play to meet her needs in ways that promote her development and learning.

The Role of Toys in Play and Learning

The kinds of toys children use in their play can influence what and how they play—that is, both the *content* and the *process* of their play. Some toys are more likely to promote higher quality play than others. Toys that are open

When children are in control of what happens and work on solving their own problems in their play, they are most likely to get the full benefits of play.

ended and unstructured—such as clay, blocks, generic toy figures, baby dolls, and stuffed animals, like Sasha's Hoppi—tend to encourage play that children can shape in their own ways to meet their needs over time.

In contrast, single-purpose, highly structured or realistic toys, such as action figures and princesses that are based on television programs or movies, can limit children's engagement in more complex, creative play.

Remote-Controlled Reading Too?

Colin, a boy in Anita's kindergarten class, told Anita she was wrong: He didn't have to learn how to read after all. He had just received a toy that read books for him. Anita later asked his parents about this "toy," and they told Anita how much they liked the electronic book system. They didn't worry about how much time Colin spent "playing" with it because it read him books, which they believed would help him learn to read. So they let him use it when they were making dinner or when they were in the car.

In recent years, as we see in the example with Colin, more and more products that claim to be toys incorporate technology in some way. These "toys" can further take control of play from children. And because children make their own meaning from their experiences, including from the toys they use, what children learn from a particular experience can be quite different from what adults think and hope they will learn. The creators of Colin's "reading toy" likely promised that it would promote reading—and this was clearly his parents' expectation—even though there is little research to support this idea. And from Colin's point of view, it freed him from the pressure he may have been feeling to learn to do so!

When children are not in control of their own play themes and the content they are imitating is violent, sexualized, or otherwise potentially concerning, one of their central avenues for growth and overall well-being—that is, creating their own play and learning through their play—can be seriously undermined. And this situation is made more worrisome because many children have less time to play now than children had in the past, as they spend more and more time using screens at home and, at school, are increasingly taught in a way that leaves little room for concrete exploration. The goal of this chapter is to help you develop a wide range of strategies for ensuring that children engage in rich and meaningful play that counteracts the restricting influence media and media culture can have, and that promotes children's optimal development and learning.

What You Can Do: Encouraging Creative, Child-Controlled Play

There is no formula or set of formulas for helping children get beyond remote-controlled play. Rather, you will need a range of strategies that can fit children's individual situations, can adapt and change with the children's interests and needs, and can evolve with the rapidly changing media and technology landscape. Here are some guidelines to help you begin or to build on what you